HBR's 10 Must Reads

UPDATED &
EXPANDED

Communication

HBR's 10 Must Reads

HBR's 10 Must Reads are definitive collections of classic ideas, practical advice, and essential thinking from the pages of *Harvard Business Review*. Exploring topics like disruptive innovation, emotional intelligence, and new technology in our ever-evolving world, these books empower any leader to make bold decisions and inspire others.

TITLES INCLUDE:

HBR's 10 Must Reads for New Managers
HBR's 10 Must Reads on Artificial Intelligence
HBR's 10 Must Reads on Building a Great Culture
HBR's 10 Must Reads on Change Management
HBR's 10 Must Reads on Communication
HBR's 10 Must Reads on Data Strategy
HBR's 10 Must Reads on Decision-Making
HBR's 10 Must Reads on Emotional Intelligence
HBR's 10 Must Reads on High Performance
HBR's 10 Must Reads on Innovation
HBR's 10 Must Reads on Leadership
HBR's 10 Must Reads on Leading Digital Transformation
HBR's 10 Must Reads on Leading Winning Teams
HBR's 10 Must Reads on Managing People
HBR's 10 Must Reads on Managing Yourself
HBR's 10 Must Reads on Marketing
HBR's 10 Must Reads on Mental Toughness
HBR's 10 Must Reads on Strategy
HBR's 10 Must Reads on Women and Leadership
HBR's 10 Must Reads Boxed Set (6 books)
HBR's 10 Must Reads Ultimate Boxed Set (14 books)

For a full list, visit hbr.org/mustreads.

HBR's 10 Must Reads

UPDATED & EXPANDED

Communication

Harvard Business Review Press
Boston, Massachusetts

Copyright 2026 Harvard Business Publishing Corporation

The web addresses referenced in this book were live and correct at the time of the book's publication but may be subject to change.

Library of Congress Cataloging-in-Publication data is forthcoming.

ISBN: 979-8-89279-298-1
eISBN: 979-8-89279-299-8

The paper used in this publication meets the requirements of the American National Standard for Permanence of Paper for Publications and Documents in Libraries and Archives Z39.48-1992.

Contents

HBR's 10 Must Reads

UPDATED & EXPANDED

Communication

1

The Necessary Art of Persuasion

by Jay A. Conger

f there ever was a time for businesspeople to learn the fine art of persuasion, it is now. Gone are the command-and-control days of executives managing by decree. Today businesses are run largely by cross-functional teams of peers and populated by baby boomers and their Generation X offspring, who show little tolerance for unquestioned authority. Electronic communication and globalization have further eroded the traditional hierarchy, as ideas and people flow more freely than ever around organizations and as decisions get made closer to the markets. These fundamental changes, more than a decade in the making but now firmly part of the economic landscape, essentially come down to this: Work today gets done in an environment where people don't just ask What should I do? but Why should I do it?

To answer this why question effectively is to persuade. Yet many businesspeople misunderstand persuasion, and more still underutilize it. The reason? Persuasion is widely perceived as a skill reserved for selling products and closing deals. It is also commonly seen as just another form of manipulation—devious and to be avoided. Certainly, persuasion can be used in selling and deal-clinching situations, and it can be misused to manipulate people. But exercised constructively and to its full potential, persuasion supersedes sales and is quite the opposite of deception. Effective persuasion becomes a negotiating and learning process through which a persuader leads colleagues to a problem's shared solution. Persuasion does indeed involve moving people to a position they don't currently hold, but not by begging or cajoling. Instead, it involves careful preparation, the proper framing of arguments, the presentation of vivid supporting evidence, and the effort to find the correct emotional match with your audience.

Effective persuasion is a difficult and time-consuming proposition, but it may also be more powerful than the command-and-control managerial model it succeeds. As AlliedSignal's CEO Lawrence Bossidy said recently, "The day when you could yell and scream and beat people into good performance is over. Today you have to appeal to them by helping them see how they can get from here to there, by establishing some credibility, and by giving them some reason and help to get there. Do all those things, and they'll knock down doors." In essence, he is describing persuasion—now more than ever, the language of business leadership.

Think for a moment of your definition of persuasion. If you are like most businesspeople I have encountered, you see persuasion as a relatively straightforward process. First, you strongly state your position. Second, you outline the supporting arguments, followed by a highly assertive, data-based exposition. Finally, you enter the deal-making stage and work toward a

Idea in Brief

This article defines and explains the four essential elements of persuasion. Business today is largely run by teams and populated by authority-averse baby boomers and Generation Xers. That makes persuasion more important than ever as a managerial tool. But contrary to popular belief, author Jay Conger (director of the University of Southern California's Marshall Business School's Leadership Institute) asserts, persuasion is not the same as selling an idea or convincing opponents to see things your way. It is instead a process of learning from others and negotiating a shared solution. To that end, persuasion consists of these essential elements: establishing credibility, framing to find common ground, providing vivid evidence, and connecting emotionally. Credibility grows, the author says, out of two sources: expertise and relationships. The former is a function of product or process knowledge and the latter a history of listening to and working in the best interest of others. But even if a persuader's credibility is high, his position must make sense—even more, it must appeal—to the audience. Therefore, a persuader must frame his position to illuminate its benefits to everyone who will feel its impact. Persuasion then becomes a matter of presenting evidence—but not just ordinary charts and spreadsheets. The author says the most effective persuaders use vivid—even over-the-top—stories, metaphors, and examples to make their positions come alive. Finally, good persuaders have the ability to accurately sense and respond to their audience's emotional state. Sometimes, that means they have to suppress their own emotions; at other times, they must intensify them. Persuasion can be a force for enormous good in an organization, but people must understand it for what it is: an often painstaking process that requires insight, planning, and compromise.

"close." In other words, you use logic, persistence, and personal enthusiasm to get others to buy a good idea. The reality is that following this process is one surefire way to fail at persuasion. (See the sidebar "Four Ways Not to Persuade.")

What, then, constitutes effective persuasion? If persuasion is a learning and negotiating process, then in the most general terms it involves phases of discovery, preparation, and dialogue.

Getting ready to persuade colleagues can take weeks or months of planning as you learn about your audience and the position you intend to argue. Before they even start to talk, effective persuaders have considered their positions from every angle. What investments in time and money will my position require from others? Is my supporting evidence weak in any way? Are there alternative positions I need to examine?

Dialogue happens before and during the persuasion process. Before the process begins, effective persuaders use dialogue to learn more about their audience's opinions, concerns, and perspectives. During the process, dialogue continues to be a form of learning, but it is also the beginning of the negotiation stage. You invite people to discuss, even debate, the merits of your position, and then to offer honest feedback and suggest alternative solutions. That may sound like a slow way to achieve your goal, but effective persuasion is about testing and revising ideas in concert with your colleagues' concerns and needs. In fact, the best persuaders not only listen to others but also incorporate their perspectives into a shared solution.

Persuasion, in other words, often involves—indeed, demands—compromise. Perhaps that is why the most effective persuaders seem to share a common trait: they are open-minded, never dogmatic. They enter the persuasion process prepared to adjust their viewpoints and incorporate others' ideas. That approach to persuasion is, interestingly, highly persuasive in itself. When colleagues see that a persuader is eager to hear their views and willing to make changes in response to their needs and concerns, they respond very positively. They trust the persuader more and listen more attentively. They don't fear being bowled over or manipulated. They see the persuader as flexible and are thus more willing to make sacrifices themselves. Because that is such a powerful dynamic, good persuaders often enter the persuasion process with judicious compromises already prepared.

Four Essential Steps

Effective persuasion involves four distinct and essential steps. First, effective persuaders establish credibility. Second, they frame their goals in a way that identifies common ground with those they intend to persuade. Third, they reinforce their positions using vivid language and compelling evidence. And fourth, they connect emotionally with their audience. As one of the most effective executives in our research commented, "The most valuable lesson I've learned about persuasion over the years is that there's just as much strategy in how you present your position as in the position itself. In fact, I'd say the strategy of presentation is the more critical."

Establish credibility

The first hurdle persuaders must overcome is their own credibility. A persuader can't advocate a new or contrarian position without having people wonder, "Can we trust this individual's perspectives and opinions?" Such a reaction is understandable. After all, allowing oneself to be persuaded is risky, because any new initiative demands a commitment of time and resources. Yet even though persuaders must have high credibility, our research strongly suggests that most managers overestimate their own credibility—considerably.

In the workplace, credibility grows out of two sources: expertise and relationships. People are considered to have high levels of

Four Ways Not to Persuade

In my work with managers as a researcher and as a consultant, I have had the unfortunate opportunity to see executives fail miserably at persuasion. Here are the four most common mistakes people make:

1. *They attempt to make their case with an up-front, hard sell.* I call this the John Wayne approach. Managers strongly state their position at the outset, and then through a process of persistence, logic, and exuberance, they try to push the idea to a close. In reality, setting out a strong position at the start of a persuasion effort gives potential opponents something to grab onto—and fight against. It's far better to present your position with the finesse and reserve of a lion tamer, who engages his "partner" by showing him the legs of a chair. In other words, effective persuaders don't begin the process by giving their colleagues a clear target in which to set their jaws.

2. *They resist compromise.* Too many managers see compromise as surrender, but it is essential to constructive persuasion. Before people buy into a proposal, they want to see that the persuader is flexible enough to respond to their concerns. Compromises can often lead to better, more sustainable shared solutions.

expertise if they have a history of sound judgment or have proven themselves knowledgeable and well informed about their proposals. For example, in proposing a new product idea, an effective persuader would need to be perceived as possessing a thorough understanding of the product—its specifications, target markets, customers, and competing products. A history of prior successes would further strengthen the persuader's perceived expertise. One extremely successful executive in our research had a track record of 14 years of devising highly effective advertising

By not compromising, ineffective persuaders unconsciously send the message that they think persuasion is a one-way street. But persuasion is a process of give-and-take. Kathleen Reardon, a professor of organizational behavior at the University of Southern California, points out that a persuader rarely changes another person's behavior or viewpoint without altering their own in the process. To persuade meaningfully, we must not only listen to others but also incorporate their perspectives into our own.

3. *They think the secret of persuasion lies in presenting great arguments.* In persuading people to change their minds, great arguments matter. No doubt about it. But arguments, per se, are only one part of the equation. Other factors matter just as much, such as the persuader's credibility and his or her ability to create a proper, mutually beneficial frame for a position, connect on the right emotional level with an audience, and communicate through vivid language that makes arguments come alive.

4. *They assume persuasion is a one-shot effort.* Persuasion is a process, not an event. Rarely, if ever, is it possible to arrive at a shared solution on the first try. More often than not, persuasion involves listening to people, testing a position, developing a new position that reflects input from the group, more testing, incorporating compromises, and then trying again. If this sounds like a slow and difficult process, that's because it is. But the results are worth the effort.

campaigns. Not surprisingly, he had an easy time winning colleagues over to his position. Another manager had a track record of seven successful new-product launches in a period of five years. He, too, had an advantage when it came to persuading his colleagues to support his next new idea.

On the relationship side, people with high credibility have demonstrated—again, usually over time—that they can be trusted to listen and to work in the best interests of others. They have also consistently shown strong emotional character and integrity; that is, they are not known for mood extremes or inconsistent performance. Indeed, people who are known to be honest, steady, and reliable have an edge when going into any persuasion situation. Because their relationships are robust, they are more apt to be given the benefit of the doubt. One effective persuader in our research was considered by colleagues to be remarkably trustworthy and fair; many people confided in her. In addition, she generously shared credit for good ideas and provided staff with exposure to the company's senior executives. This woman had built strong relationships, which meant her staff and peers were always willing to consider seriously what she proposed.

If expertise and relationships determine credibility, it is crucial that you undertake an honest assessment of where you stand on both criteria before beginning to persuade. To do so, first step back and ask yourself the following questions related to expertise: How will others perceive my knowledge about the strategy, product, or change I am proposing? Do I have a track record in this area that others know about and respect? Then, to assess the strength of your relationship credibility, ask yourself, Do those I am hoping to persuade see me as helpful, trustworthy, and supportive? Will they see me as someone in sync with them— emotionally, intellectually, and politically—on issues like this one? Finally, it is important to note that it is not enough to get your own read on these matters. You must also test your answers with colleagues you trust to give you a reality check. Only then will you have a complete picture of your credibility.

In most cases, that exercise helps people discover that they have some measure of weakness, either on the expertise or on the relationship side of credibility. The challenge then becomes to fill in such gaps.

In general, if your area of weakness is on the expertise side, you have several options:

- First, you can learn more about the complexities of your position through either formal or informal education and through conversations with knowledgeable individuals. You might also get more relevant experience on the job by asking, for instance, to be assigned to a team that would increase your insight into particular markets or products.

- Another alternative is to hire someone to bolster your expertise—for example, an industry consultant or a recognized outside expert, such as a professor. Either one may have the knowledge and experience required to support your position effectively. Similarly, you may tap experts within your organization to advocate your position. Their credibility becomes a substitute for your own.

- You can also utilize other outside sources of information to support your position, such as respected business or trade periodicals, books, independently produced reports, and lectures by experts. In our research, one executive from the clothing industry successfully persuaded his company to reposition an entire product line to a more youthful market after bolstering his credibility with articles by a noted demographer in two highly regarded journals and with two independent market-research studies.

- Finally, you may launch pilot projects to demonstrate on a small scale your expertise and the value of your ideas.

As for filling in the relationship gap:

- You should make a concerted effort to meet one-on-one with all the key people you plan to persuade. This is not the time to outline your position but rather to get a range of perspectives on the issue at hand. If you have the time and resources, you should even offer to help these people with issues that concern them.

- Another option is to involve like-minded coworkers who already have strong relationships with your audience. Again, that is a matter of seeking out substitutes on your own behalf.

For an example of how these strategies can be put to work, consider the case of a chief operating officer of a large retail bank, whom we will call Tom Smith. Although he was new to his job, Smith ardently wanted to persuade the senior management team that the company was in serious trouble. He believed that the bank's overhead was excessive and would jeopardize its position as the industry entered a more competitive era. Most of his colleagues, however, did not see the potential seriousness of the situation. Because the bank had been enormously successful in recent years, they believed changes in the industry posed little danger. In addition to being newly appointed, Smith had another problem: His career had been in financial services, and he was considered an outsider in the world of retail banking. Thus he had few personal connections to draw on as he made his case, nor was he perceived to be particularly knowledgeable about marketplace exigencies.

As a first step in establishing credibility, Smith hired an external consultant with respected credentials in the industry who showed that the bank was indeed poorly positioned to be a low-cost producer. In a series of interactive presentations to the bank's top-level management, the consultant revealed how the company's leading competitors were taking aggressive actions to contain operating costs. He made it clear from these presentations that not cutting costs would soon cause the bank to fall drastically behind the competition. These findings were then distributed in written reports that circulated throughout the bank.

Next, Smith determined that the bank's branch managers were critical to his campaign. The buy-in of those respected and informed individuals would signal to others in the company that his concerns were valid. Moreover, Smith looked to the branch managers because he believed that they could increase his expertise about marketplace trends and also help him test his own assumptions. Thus, for the next three months, he visited every branch in his region of Ontario, Canada—135 in all. During each visit, he spent time with branch managers, listening to their perceptions of the bank's strengths and weaknesses. He learned firsthand about the competition's initiatives and customer trends, and he solicited ideas for improving the bank's services and minimizing costs. By the time he was through, Smith had a broad perspective on the bank's future that few people even in senior management possessed. And he had built dozens of relationships in the process.

Finally, Smith launched some small but highly visible initiatives to demonstrate his expertise and capabilities. For example, he was concerned about slow growth in the company's mortgage business and the loan officers' resulting slip in morale. So he devised a program in which new mortgage customers would make no payments for the first 90 days. The initiative proved remarkably successful, and in short order Smith appeared to be a far more savvy retail banker than anyone had assumed.

Another example of how to establish credibility comes from Microsoft. In 1990, two product-development managers, Karen Fries and Barry Linnett, came to believe that the market would greatly welcome software that featured a "social interface." They envisioned a package that would employ animated human and animal characters to show users how to go about their computing tasks.

Inside Microsoft, however, employees had immediate concerns about the concept. Software programmers ridiculed the cute characters. Animated characters had been used before only in software for children, making their use in adult environments hard to envision. But Fries and Linnett felt their proposed product had both dynamism and complexity, and they remained convinced that consumers would eagerly buy such programs. They also believed that the home-computer software market—largely untapped at the time and with fewer software standards—would be open to such innovation.

Within the company, Fries had gained quite a bit of relationship credibility. She had started out as a recruiter for the company in 1987 and had worked directly for many of Microsoft's senior executives. They trusted and liked her. In addition, she had been responsible for hiring the company's product and program managers. As a result, she knew all the senior people at Microsoft and had hired many of the people who would be deciding on her product.

Linnett's strength lay in his expertise. In particular, he knew the technology behind an innovative tutorial program called PC Works. In addition, both Fries and Linnett had managed Publisher, a product with a unique help feature called Wizards, which Microsoft's CEO, Bill Gates, had liked. But those factors were sufficient only to get an initial hearing from Microsoft's senior management. To persuade the organization to move forward, the pair would need to improve perceptions of their expertise. It hurt them that this type of social-interface software had no proven track record of success and that they were both novices with such software. Their challenge became one of finding substitutes for their own expertise.

Their first step was a wise one. From within Microsoft, they hired respected technical guru Darrin Massena. With Massena, they developed a set of prototypes to demonstrate that they did indeed understand the software's technology and could make it work. They then tested the prototypes in market research, and users responded enthusiastically. Finally, and most important, they enlisted two Stanford University professors, Clifford Nass and Byron Reeves, both experts in human-computer interaction. In several meetings with Microsoft senior managers and Gates himself, they presented a rigorously compiled and thorough body of research that demonstrated how and why social-interface software was ideally suited to the average computer user. In addition, Fries and Linnett asserted that considerable jumps in computing power would make more realistic cartoon characters an increasingly malleable technology. Their product, they said, was the leading edge of an incipient software revolution. Convinced, Gates approved a full product-development team, and in January 1995, the product called BOB was launched. BOB went on to sell more than half a million copies, and its concept and technology are being used within Microsoft as a platform for developing several Internet products.

Credibility is the cornerstone of effective persuading; without it, a persuader won't be given the time of day. In the best-case scenario, people enter into a persuasion situation with some measure of expertise and relationship credibility. But it is important to note that credibility along either lines can be built or bought. Indeed, it must be, or the next steps are an exercise in futility.

Frame for common ground

Even if your credibility is high, your position must still appeal strongly to the people you are trying to persuade. After all, few people will jump on board a train that will bring them to ruin or even mild discomfort. Effective persuaders must be adept at describing their positions in terms that illuminate their advantages. As any parent can tell you, the fastest way to get a child to come along willingly on a trip to the grocery store is to point out that there are lollipops by the cash register. That is not deception. It is just a persuasive way of framing the benefits of taking such a journey. In work situations, persuasive framing is obviously more complex, but the underlying principle is the same. It is a process of identifying shared benefits.

Monica Ruffo, an account executive for an advertising agency, offers a good example of persuasive framing. Her client, a fast-food chain, was instituting a promotional campaign in Canada; menu items such as a hamburger, fries, and cola were to be bundled together and sold at a low price. The strategy made sense to corporate headquarters. Its research showed that consumers thought the company's products were higher priced than the competition's, and the company was anxious to overcome this perception. The franchisees, on the other hand, were still experiencing strong sales and were far more concerned about the short-term impact that the new, low prices would have on their profit margins.

A less experienced persuader would have attempted to rationalize headquarters' perspective to the franchisees—to convince them of its validity. But Ruffo framed the change in pricing to demonstrate its benefits to the franchisees themselves. The new value campaign, she explained, would actually improve franchisees' profits. To back up this point, she drew on several sources. A pilot project in Tennessee, for instance, had demonstrated that under the new pricing scheme, the sales of french fries and drinks—the two most profitable items on the menu—had markedly increased. In addition, the company had rolled out medium-sized meal packages in 80% of its U.S. outlets, and franchisees' sales of fries and drinks had jumped 26%. Citing research from a respected business periodical, Ruffo also showed that when customers raised their estimate of the value they receive from a retail establishment by 10%, the establishment's sales rose by 1%. She had estimated that the new meal plan would increase value perceptions by 100%, with the result that franchisee sales could be expected to grow 10%.

Ruffo closed her presentation with a letter written many years before by the company's founder to the organization. It was an emotional letter extolling the values of the company and stressing the importance of the franchisees to the company's success. It also highlighted the importance of the company's position as the low-price leader in the industry. The beliefs and values contained in the letter had long been etched in the minds of Ruffo's audience. Hearing them again only confirmed the company's concern for the franchisees and the importance of their winning formula. They also won Ruffo a standing ovation. That day, the franchisees voted unanimously to support the new meal-pricing plan.

The Ruffo case illustrates why—in choosing appropriate positioning—it is critical first to identify your objective's tangible benefits to the people you are trying to persuade. Sometimes that is easy. Mutual benefits exist. In other situations, however, no shared advantages are readily apparent—or meaningful. In these cases, effective persuaders adjust their positions. They know it is impossible to engage people and gain commitment to ideas or plans without highlighting the advantages to all the parties involved.

At the heart of framing is a solid understanding of your audience. Even before starting to persuade, the best persuaders we have encountered closely study the issues that matter to their colleagues. They use conversations, meetings, and other forms of dialogue to collect essential information. They are good at listening. They test their ideas with trusted confidants, and they ask questions of the people they will later be persuading. Those steps help them think through the arguments, the evidence, and the perspectives they will present. Oftentimes, this process causes them to alter or compromise their own plans before they even start persuading. It is through this thoughtful, inquisitive approach they develop frames that appeal to their audience.

Consider the case of a manager who was in charge of process engineering for a jet engine manufacturer. He had redesigned the work flow for routine turbine maintenance for airline clients in a manner that would dramatically shorten the turnaround time for servicing. Before presenting his ideas to the company's president, he consulted a good friend in the company, the vice president of engineering, who knew the president well. This conversation revealed that the president's prime concern would not be speed or efficiency but profitability. To get the president's buy-in, the vice president explained, the new system would have to improve the company's profitability in the short run by lowering operating expenses.

At first this information had the manager stumped. He had planned to focus on efficiency and had even intended to request additional funding to make the process work. But his conversation with the vice president sparked him to change his position. Indeed, he went so far as to change the workflow design itself so that it no longer required new investment but rather drove down costs. He then carefully documented the cost savings and profitability gains that his new plan would produce and presented this revised plan to the president. With his initiative positioned anew, the manager persuaded the president and got the project approved.

Provide evidence

With credibility established and a common frame identified, persuasion becomes a matter of presenting evidence. Ordinary evidence, however, won't do. We have found that the most effective persuaders use language in a particular way. They supplement numerical data with examples, stories, metaphors, and analogies to make their positions come alive. That use of language paints a vivid word picture and, in doing so, lends a compelling and tangible quality to the persuader's point of view.

Think about a typical persuasion situation. The persuader is often advocating a goal, strategy, or initiative with an uncertain outcome. Karen Fries and Barry Linnett, for instance, wanted Microsoft to invest millions of dollars in a software package with chancy technology and unknown market demand. The team could have supported its case solely with market research, financial projections, and the like. But that would have been a mistake, because research shows that most people perceive such reports as not entirely informative. They are too abstract to be completely meaningful or memorable. In essence, the numbers don't make an emotional impact.

By contrast, stories and vivid language do, particularly when they present comparable situations to the one under discussion.

A marketing manager trying to persuade senior executives to invest in a new product, for example, might cite examples of similar investments that paid off handsomely. Indeed, we found that people readily draw lessons from such cases. More important, the research shows that listeners absorb information in proportion to its vividness. Thus it is no wonder that Fries and Linnett hit a home run when they presented their case for BOB with the following analogy:

> *Imagine you want to cook dinner and you must first go to the supermarket. You have all the flexibility you want— you can cook anything in the world as long as you know how and have the time and desire to do it. When you arrive at the supermarket, you find all these overstuffed aisles with cryptic single-word headings like "sundries" and "ethnic food" and "condiments." These are the menus on typical computer interfaces. The question is whether salt is under condiments or ethnic food or near the potato chip section. There are surrounding racks and wall spaces, much as our software interfaces now have support buttons, toolbars, and lines around the perimeters. Now after you have collected everything, you still need to put it all together in the correct order to make a meal. If you're a good cook, your meal will probably be good. If you're a novice, it probably won't be.*
>
> *We [at Microsoft] have been selling under the supermarket category for years, and we think there is a big opportunity for restaurants. That's what we are trying to do now with BOB: pushing the next step with software that is more like going to a restaurant, so the user doesn't spend all of his time searching for the ingredients. We find and put the*

ingredients together. You sit down, you get comfortable. We bring you a menu. We do the work, you relax. It's an enjoyable experience. No walking around lost trying to find things, no cooking.

Had Fries and Linnett used a literal description of BOB's advantages, few of their highly computer-literate colleagues at Microsoft would have personally related to the menu-searching frustration that BOB was designed to eliminate. The analogy they selected, however, made BOB's purpose both concrete and memorable.

A master persuader, Mary Kay Ash, the founder of Mary Kay Cosmetics, regularly draws on analogies to illustrate and "sell" the business conduct she values. Consider this speech at the company's annual sales convention:

Back in the days of the Roman Empire, the legions of the emperor conquered the known world. There was, however, one band of people that the Romans never conquered. Those people were the followers of the great teacher from Bethlehem. Historians have long since discovered that one of the reasons for the sturdiness of this folk was their habit of meeting together weekly. They shared their difficulties, and they stood side by side. Does this remind you of something? The way we stand side by side and share our knowledge and difficulties with each other in our weekly unit meetings? I have so often observed when a director or unit member is confronted with a personal problem that the unit stands together in helping that sister in distress. What a wonderful circle of friendships we have. Perhaps it's one of the greatest fringe benefits of our company.

Through her vivid analogy, Ash links collective support in the company to a courageous period in Christian history. In doing so, she accomplishes several objectives. First, she drives home her belief that collective support is crucial to the success of the organization. Most Mary Kay salespeople are independent operators who face the daily challenges of direct selling. An emotional support system of fellow salespeople is essential to ensure that self-esteem and confidence remain intact in the face of rejection. Next she suggests by her analogy that solidarity against the odds is the best way to stymie powerful oppressors—to wit, the competition. Finally, Ash's choice of analogy imbues a sense of a heroic mission to the work of her sales force.

You probably don't need to invoke the analogy of the Christian struggle to support your position, but effective persuaders are not afraid of unleashing the immense power of language. In fact, they use it to their utmost advantage.

Connect emotionally

In the business world, we like to think that our colleagues use reason to make their decisions, yet if we scratch below the surface we will always find emotions at play. Good persuaders are aware of the primacy of emotions and are responsive to them in two important ways. First, they show their own emotional commitment to the position they are advocating. Such expression is a delicate matter. If you act too emotional, people may doubt your clearheadedness. But you must also show that your commitment to a goal is not just in your mind but in your heart and gut as well. Without this demonstration of feeling, people may wonder if you actually believe in the position you're championing.

Perhaps more important, however, is that effective persuaders have a strong and accurate sense of their audience's emotional state, and they adjust the tone of their arguments accordingly. Sometimes that means coming on strong, with forceful points. Other times, a whisper may be all that is required. The idea is that whatever your position, you match your emotional fervor to your audience's ability to receive the message.

Effective persuaders seem to have a second sense about how their colleagues have interpreted past events in the organization and how they will probably interpret a proposal. The best persuaders in our study would usually canvass key individuals who had a good pulse on the mood and emotional expectations of those about to be persuaded. They would ask those individuals how various proposals might affect colleagues on an emotional level—in essence, testing possible reactions. They were also quite effective at gathering information through informal conversations in the hallways or at lunch. In the end, their aim was to ensure that the emotional appeal behind their persuasion matched what their audience was already feeling or expecting.

To illustrate the importance of emotional matchmaking in persuasion, consider this example. The president of an aeronautics manufacturing company strongly believed that the maintenance costs and turnaround time of the company's U.S. and foreign competitors were so much better than his own company's that it stood to lose customers and profits. He wanted to communicate his fear and his urgent desire for change to his senior managers. So one afternoon, he called them into the boardroom. On an overhead screen was the projected image of a smiling man flying an old-fashioned biplane with his scarf blowing in the wind. The right half of the transparency was covered. When everyone was seated, the president explained that he felt as this pilot did, given the company's recent good fortune. The organization, after all, had just finished its most successful year in history. But then with a deep sigh, he announced that his happiness was quickly vanishing. As the president lifted the remaining portion of the sheet, he revealed an image of the pilot flying directly into a wall. The president then faced his audience and in a heavy voice said, "This is what I see happening to us." He asserted that the company was headed for a crash if people didn't take action fast. He then went on to lecture the group about the steps needed to counter this threat.

The reaction from the group was immediate and negative. Directly after the meeting, managers gathered in small clusters in the hallways to talk about the president's "scare tactics." They resented what they perceived to be the president's overstatement of the case. As the managers saw it, they had exerted enormous effort that year to break the company's records in sales and profitability. They were proud of their achievements. In fact, they had entered the meeting expecting it would be the moment of recognition. But to their absolute surprise, they were scolded.

The president's mistake? First, he should have canvassed a few members of his senior team to ascertain the emotional state of the group. From that, he would have learned that they were in need of thanks and recognition. He should then have held a separate session devoted simply to praising the team's accomplishments. Later, in a second meeting, he could have expressed his own anxieties about the coming year. And rather than blame the team for ignoring the future, he could have calmly described what he saw as emerging threats to the company and then asked his management team to help him develop new initiatives.

Now let us look at someone who found the right emotional match with his audience: Robert Marcell, head of Chrysler's small-car design team. In the early 1990s, Chrysler was eager to produce a new subcompact—indeed, the company had not introduced a new model of this type since 1978. But senior managers at Chrysler did not want to go it alone. They thought an alliance with a foreign manufacturer would improve the car's design and protect Chrysler's cash stores.

Marcell was convinced otherwise. He believed that the company should bring the design and production of a new subcompact in-house. He knew that persuading senior managers would be difficult, but he also had his own team to contend with. Team members had lost their confidence that they would ever again have the opportunity to create a good car. They were also angry that the United States had once again given up its position to foreign competitors when it came to small cars.

Marcell decided that his persuasion tactics had to be built around emotional themes that would touch his audience. From innumerable conversations around the company, he learned that many people felt as he did—that to surrender the subcompact's design to a foreign manufacturer was to surrender the company's soul and, ultimately, its ability to provide jobs. In addition, he felt deeply that his organization was a talented group hungry for a challenge and an opportunity to restore its self-esteem and pride. He would need to demonstrate his faith in the team's abilities.

Marcell prepared a 15-minute talk built around slides of his hometown, Iron River, a now defunct mining town in Upper Michigan, devastated, in large part, by foreign mining companies. On the screen flashed recent photographs he had taken of his boarded-up high school, the shuttered homes of his childhood friends, the crumbling ruins of the town's ironworks, closed churches, and an abandoned railroad yard. After a description of each of these places, he said the phrase, "We couldn't compete"—like the refrain of a hymn. Marcell's point was that the same outcome awaited Detroit if the production of small cars was not brought back to the United States. Surrender was the enemy, he said, and devastation would follow if the group did not take immediate action.

Marcell ended his slide show on a hopeful note. He spoke of his pride in his design group and then challenged the team to build a "made-in-America" subcompact that would prove that the United States could still compete. The speech, which echoed the exact sentiments of the audience, rekindled the group's fighting spirit. Shortly after the speech, group members began drafting their ideas for a new car.

Marcell then took his slide show to the company's senior management and ultimately to Chrysler chairman Lee Iacocca. As Marcell showed his slides, he could see that Iacocca was touched. Iacocca, after all, was a fighter and a strongly patriotic man himself. In fact, Marcell's approach was not too different from Iacocca's earlier appeal to the United States Congress to save Chrysler. At the end of the show, Marcell stopped and said, "If we dare to be different, we could be the reason the U.S. auto industry survives. We could be the reason our kids and grandkids don't end up working at fast-food chains." Iacocca stayed on for two hours as Marcell explained in greater detail what his team was planning. Afterward, Iacocca changed his mind and gave Marcell's group approval to develop a car, the Neon.

With both groups, Marcell skillfully matched his emotional tenor to that of the group he was addressing. The ideas he conveyed resonated deeply with his largely Midwestern audience. And rather than leave them in a depressed state, he offered them hope, which was more persuasive than promising doom. Again, this played to the strong patriotic sentiments of his American-heartland audience.

No effort to persuade can succeed without emotion, but showing too much emotion can be as unproductive as showing too little. The important point to remember is that you must match your emotions to your audience's.

The Force of Persuasion

The concept of persuasion, like that of power, often confuses and even mystifies businesspeople. It is so complex—and so dangerous when mishandled—that many would rather just avoid it altogether. But like power, persuasion can be a force for enormous good in an organization. It can pull people together, move ideas forward, galvanize change, and forge constructive solutions. To do all that, however, people must understand persuasion for what it is—not convincing and selling but learning and negotiating. Furthermore, it must be seen as an art form that requires commitment and practice, especially as today's business contingencies make persuasion more necessary than ever.

Originally published in May–June 1998. Reprint 98304

2

The Surprising Power of Questions

by Alison Wood Brooks and Leslie K. John

Much of an executive's workday is spent asking others for information—requesting status updates from a team leader, for example, or questioning a counterpart in a tense negotiation. Yet unlike professionals such as litigators, journalists, and doctors, who are taught how to ask questions as an essential part of their training, few executives think of questioning as a skill that can be honed—or consider how their own answers to questions could make conversations more productive.

That's a missed opportunity. Questioning is a uniquely powerful tool for unlocking value in organizations: It spurs learning and the exchange of ideas, it fuels innovation and performance improvement, it builds rapport and trust among team members. And it can mitigate business risk by uncovering unforeseen pitfalls and hazards.

For some people, questioning comes easily. Their natural inquis-itiveness, emotional intelligence, and ability to read people put the ideal question on the tip of their tongue. But most of us don't ask enough questions, nor do we pose our inquiries in an optimal way.

The good news is that by asking questions, we naturally improve our emotional intelligence, which in turn makes us better questioners—a virtuous cycle. In this article, we draw on insights from behavioral science research to explore how the way we frame questions and choose to answer our counterparts can influence the outcome of conversations. We offer guidance for choosing the best type, tone, sequence, and framing of ques-tions and for deciding what and how much information to share to reap the most benefit from our interactions, not just for our-selves but for our organizations.

Don't Ask, Don't Get

"Be a good listener," Dale Carnegie advised in his 1936 classic *How to Win Friends and Influence People.* "Ask questions the other person will enjoy answering." More than 80 years later, most people still fail to heed Carnegie's sage advice. When one of us (Alison) began studying conversations at Harvard Business School several years ago, she quickly arrived at a foundational insight: People don't ask enough questions. In fact, among the most common complaints people make after having a conver-sation, such as an interview, a first date, or a work meeting, is "I wish [s/he] had asked me more questions" and "I can't believe [s/he] didn't ask me any questions."

Why do so many of us hold back? There are many reasons. People may be egocentric—eager to impress others with their own thoughts, stories, and ideas (and not even think to ask questions).

Idea in Brief

The Problem

Some professionals such as litigators, journalists, and even doctors are taught to ask questions as part of their training. But few executives think about questioning as a skill that can be honed. That's a missed opportunity.

The Opportunity

Questioning is a powerful tool for unlocking value in companies: It spurs learning and the exchange of ideas, it fuels innovation and better performance, and it builds trust among team members. And it can mitigate business risk by uncovering unforeseen pitfalls and hazards.

The Approach

Several techniques can enhance the power and efficacy of queries: Favor follow-up questions, know when to keep questions open-ended, get the sequence right, use the right tone, and pay attention to group dynamics.

Perhaps they are apathetic—they don't care enough to ask, or they anticipate being bored by the answers they'd hear. They may be overconfident in their own knowledge and think they already know the answers (which sometimes they do, but usually not). Or perhaps they worry that they'll ask the wrong question and be viewed as rude or incompetent. But the biggest inhibitor, in our opinion, is that most people just don't understand how beneficial good questioning can be. If they did, they would end far fewer sentences with a period—and more with a question mark.

Dating back to the 1970s, research suggests that people have conversations to accomplish some combination of two major goals: information exchange (learning) and impression management (liking). Recent research shows that asking questions achieves both. Alison and Harvard colleagues Karen Huang, Michael Yeomans, Julia Minson, and Francesca Gino scrutinized thousands of natural conversations among participants who were getting to know each other, either in online chats or on in-person speed dates. The researchers told some people to ask many questions (at least nine in fifteen minutes) and others to ask very few (no more than four in fifteen minutes). In the online chats, the people who were randomly assigned to ask many questions were better liked by their conversation partners and learned more about their partners' interests. For example, when quizzed about their partners' preferences for activities such as reading, cooking, and exercising, high question askers were more likely to be able to guess correctly. Among the speed daters, people were more willing to go on a second date with partners who asked more questions. In fact, asking just one more question on each date meant that participants persuaded one additional person (over the course of 20 dates) to go out with them again.

Questions are such powerful tools that they can be beneficial—perhaps particularly so—in circumstances when question asking goes against social norms. For instance, prevailing norms tell us that job candidates are expected to answer questions during interviews. But research by Dan Cable, at the London Business School, and Virginia Kay, at the University of North Carolina, suggests that most people excessively self-promote during job interviews. And when interviewees focus on selling themselves, they are likely to forget to ask questions—about the interviewer, the organization, the work—that would make the interviewer feel more engaged and more apt to view the candidate favorably and could help the candidate predict whether the job would provide satisfying work. For job candidates, asking questions such as "What am I not asking you that I should?" can signal competence, build rapport, and unlock key pieces of information about the position.

Most people don't grasp that asking a lot of questions unlocks learning and improves interpersonal bonding. In Alison's studies, for example, though people could accurately recall how many questions had been asked in their conversations, they didn't intuit the link between questions and liking. Across four studies, in which participants were engaged in conversations themselves or read transcripts of others' conversations, people tended not to realize that question asking would influence—or had influenced—the level of amity between the conversationalists.

The New Socratic Method

The first step in becoming a better questioner is simply to ask more questions. Of course, the sheer number of questions is not the only factor that influences the quality of a conversation: The type, tone, sequence, and framing also matter.

In our teaching at Harvard Business School, we run an exercise in which we instruct pairs of students to have a conversation. Some students are told to ask as few questions as possible, and some are instructed to ask as many as possible. Among the low-low pairs (both students ask a minimum of questions), participants generally report that the experience is a bit like children engaging in parallel play: They exchange statements but struggle to initiate an interactive, enjoyable, or productive dialogue. The high-high pairs find that too many questions can also create a stilted dynamic. However, the high-low pairs' experiences are mixed. Sometimes the question asker learns a lot about her partner, the answerer feels heard, and both come away feeling profoundly closer. Other times, one of the participants may feel uncomfortable in his role or unsure about how much to share, and the conversation can feel like an interrogation.

Our research suggests several approaches that can enhance the power and efficacy of queries. The best approach for a given situation depends on the goals of the conversationalists—specifically, whether the discussion is cooperative (for example, the duo is trying to build a relationship or accomplish a task together) or competitive (the parties seek to uncover sensitive information from each other or serve their own interests), or some combination of both. (See the exhibit "Conversational goals matter.") Consider the following tactics.

Favor follow-up questions

Not all questions are created equal. Alison's research, using human coding and machine learning, revealed four types of questions: introductory questions ("How are you?"), mirror questions ("I'm fine. How are you?"), full-switch questions (ones that change the topic entirely), and follow-up questions (ones that solicit more information). Although each type is abundant in natural conversation, follow-up questions seem to have special power. They signal to your conversation partner that you are listening, care, and want to know more. People interacting with a partner who asks lots of follow-up questions tend to feel respected and heard.

An unexpected benefit of follow-up questions is that they don't require much thought or preparation—indeed, they seem to come naturally to interlocutors. In Alison's studies, the people who were told to ask more questions used more follow-up questions than any other type without being instructed to do so.

Know when to keep questions open-ended

No one likes to feel interrogated—and some types of questions can force answerers into a yes-or-no corner. Open-ended questions can counteract that effect and thus can be particularly useful in

Conversational goals matter

Conversations fall along a continuum from purely competitive to purely cooperative. For example, discussions about the allocation of scarce resources tend to be competitive; those between friends and colleagues are generally cooperative; and others, such as managers' check-ins with employees, are mixed—supportive but also providing feedback and communicating expectations. Here are some challenges that commonly arise when asking and answering questions and tactics for handling them.

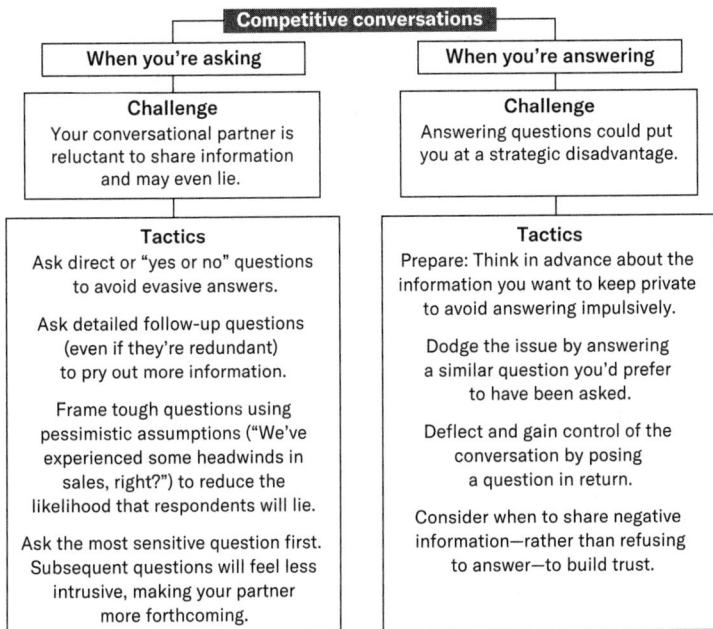

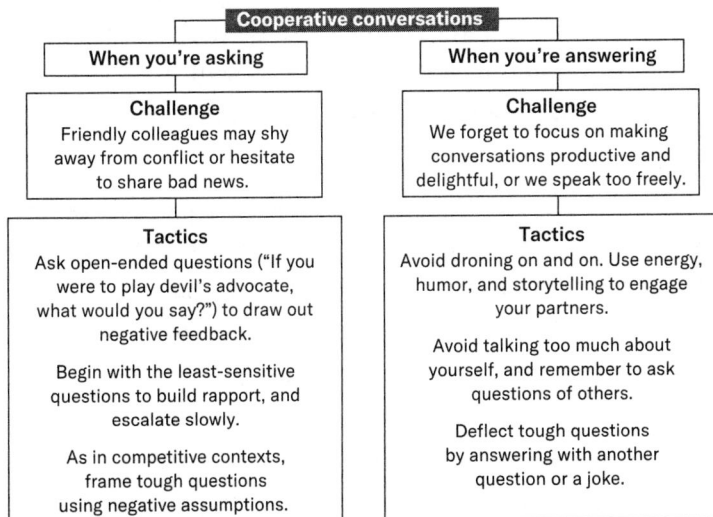

Competitive conversations

When you're asking

Challenge
Your conversational partner is reluctant to share information and may even lie.

Tactics
Ask direct or "yes or no" questions to avoid evasive answers.

Ask detailed follow-up questions (even if they're redundant) to pry out more information.

Frame tough questions using pessimistic assumptions ("We've experienced some headwinds in sales, right?") to reduce the likelihood that respondents will lie.

Ask the most sensitive question first. Subsequent questions will feel less intrusive, making your partner more forthcoming.

When you're answering

Challenge
Answering questions could put you at a strategic disadvantage.

Tactics
Prepare: Think in advance about the information you want to keep private to avoid answering impulsively.

Dodge the issue by answering a similar question you'd prefer to have been asked.

Deflect and gain control of the conversation by posing a question in return.

Consider when to share negative information—rather than refusing to answer—to build trust.

Cooperative conversations

When you're asking

Challenge
Friendly colleagues may shy away from conflict or hesitate to share bad news.

Tactics
Ask open-ended questions ("If you were to play devil's advocate, what would you say?") to draw out negative feedback.

Begin with the least-sensitive questions to build rapport, and escalate slowly.

As in competitive contexts, frame tough questions using negative assumptions.

When you're answering

Challenge
We forget to focus on making conversations productive and delightful, or we speak too freely.

Tactics
Avoid droning on and on. Use energy, humor, and storytelling to engage your partners.

Avoid talking too much about yourself, and remember to ask questions of others.

Deflect tough questions by answering with another question or a joke.

uncovering information or learning something new. Indeed, they are wellsprings of innovation—which is often the result of finding the hidden, unexpected answer that no one has thought of before.

A wealth of research in survey design has shown the dangers of narrowing respondents' options. For example, "closed" questions can introduce bias and manipulation. In one study, in which parents were asked what they deemed "the most important thing for children to prepare them in life," about 60% of them chose "to think for themselves" from a list of response options. However, when the same question was asked in an open-ended format, only about 5% of parents spontaneously came up with an answer along those lines.

Of course, open-ended questions aren't always optimal. For example, if you are in a tense negotiation or are dealing with people who tend to keep their cards close to their chest, open-ended questions can leave too much wiggle room, inviting them to dodge or lie by omission. In such situations, closed questions work better, especially if they are framed correctly. For example, research by Julia Minson, the University of Utah's Eric VanEpps, Georgetown's Jeremy Yip, and Wharton's Maurice Schweitzer indicates that people are less likely to lie if questioners make pessimistic assumptions ("This business will need some new equipment soon, correct?") rather than optimistic ones ("The equipment is in good working order, right?").

Sometimes the information you wish to ascertain is so sensitive that direct questions won't work, no matter how thoughtfully they are framed. In these situations, a survey tactic can aid discovery. In research Leslie conducted with Alessandro Acquisti and George Loewenstein of Carnegie Mellon University, she found that people were more forthcoming when requests for sensitive information were couched within another task—in the study's case, rating the ethicality of antisocial behaviors such as cheating on one's tax return or letting a drunk friend drive home. Participants were asked to rate the ethicality using one scale if they had engaged in a particular behavior and another scale if they hadn't—thus revealing which antisocial acts they themselves had engaged in. Although this tactic may sometimes prove useful at an organizational level—we can imagine that managers might administer a survey rather than ask workers directly about sensitive information such as salary expectations—we counsel restraint in using it. If people feel that you are trying to trick them into revealing something, they may lose trust in you, decreasing the likelihood that they'll share information in the future and potentially eroding workplace relationships.

Get the sequence right

The optimal order of your questions depends on the circumstances. During tense encounters, asking tough questions first, even if it feels socially awkward to do so, can make your conversational partner more willing to open up. Leslie and her coauthors found that people are more willing to reveal sensitive information when questions are asked in a decreasing order of intrusiveness. When a question asker begins with a highly sensitive question—such as "Have you ever had a fantasy of doing something terrible to someone?"—subsequent questions, such as "Have you ever called in sick to work when you were perfectly healthy?" feel, by comparison, less intrusive, and thus we tend to be more forthcoming. Of course, if the first question is *too* sensitive, you run the risk of offending your counterpart. So it's a delicate balance, to be sure.

If the goal is to build relationships, the opposite approach—opening with less sensitive questions and escalating slowly—seems to be most effective. In a classic set of studies (the results

The Power of Questions in Sales

There are few business settings in which asking questions is more important than sales. A recent study of more than 500,000 business-to-business sales conversations—over the phone and via online platforms—by tech company Gong.io reveals that top-performing salespeople ask questions differently than their peers.

Consistent with past research, the data shows a strong connection between the number of questions a salesperson asks and his or her sales conversion rate (in terms of both securing the next meeting and eventually closing the deal). This is true even after controlling for the gender of the salesperson and the call type (demo, proposal, negotiation, and so on). However, there is a point of diminishing returns. Conversion rates start to drop off after about 14 questions, with 11 to 14 being the optimal range.

The data also shows that top-performing salespeople tend to scatter questions throughout the sales call, which makes it feel more like a conversation than an interrogation. Lower performers, in contrast, frontload questions in the first half of the sales call, as if they're making their way through a to-do list.

Just as important, top salespeople listen more and speak less than their counterparts overall. Taken together, the data from Gong.io affirms what great salespeople intuitively understand: When sellers ask questions rather than just make their pitch, they close more deals.

of which went viral following a write-up in the "Modern Love" column of the *New York Times*), psychologist Arthur Aron recruited strangers to come to the lab, paired them up, and gave them a list of questions. They were told to work their way through the list, starting with relatively shallow inquiries and progressing to more self-revelatory ones, such as "What is your biggest regret?" Pairs in the control group were asked simply to interact with each other. The pairs who followed the prescribed structure liked each other more than the control pairs. This effect is so strong that it has been formalized in a task called "the relationship closeness induction," a tool used by researchers to build a sense of connection among experiment participants.

Good interlocutors also understand that questions asked previously in a conversation can influence future queries. For example, Norbert Schwarz, of the University of Southern California, and his coauthors found that when the question "How satisfied are you with your life?" is followed by the question "How satisfied are you with your marriage?" the answers were highly correlated: Respondents who reported being satisfied with their life also said they were satisfied with their marriage. When asked the questions in this order, people implicitly interpreted that life satisfaction "ought to be" closely tied to marriage. However, when the same questions were asked in the opposite order, the answers were less closely correlated.

Use the right tone

People are more forthcoming when you ask questions in a casual way, rather than in a buttoned-up, official tone. In one of Leslie's studies, participants were posed a series of sensitive questions in an online survey. For one group of participants, the website's user interface looked fun and frivolous; for another group, the site looked official. (The control group was presented with a neutral-looking site.) Participants were about twice as likely to reveal sensitive information on the casual-looking site than on the others.

People also tend to be more forthcoming when given an escape hatch or "out" in a conversation. For example, if they are told that they can change their answers at any point, they tend to open up more—even though they rarely end up making changes. This might explain why teams and groups find brainstorming sessions so productive. In a whiteboard setting, where anything can be erased and judgment is suspended, people are more likely to answer questions honestly and say things they otherwise might not. Of course, there will be times when an off-the-cuff approach is inappropriate. But in general, an overly formal tone is likely to inhibit people's willingness to share information.

Pay attention to group dynamics

Conversational dynamics can change profoundly depending on whether you're chatting one-on-one with someone or talking in a group. Not only is the willingness to answer questions affected simply by the presence of others, but members of a group tend to follow one another's lead. In one set of studies, Leslie and her coauthors asked participants a series of sensitive questions, including ones about finances ("Have you ever bounced a check?") and sex ("While an adult, have you ever felt sexual desire for a minor?"). Participants were told either that most others in the study were willing to reveal stigmatizing answers or that they were unwilling to do so. Participants who were told that others had been forthcoming were 27% likelier to reveal sensitive answers than those who were told that others had been reticent. In a meeting or group setting, it takes only a few closed-off people for questions to lose their probing power. The opposite is true, too. As soon as one person starts to open up, the rest of the group is likely to follow suit.

Group dynamics can also affect how a question asker is perceived. Alison's research reveals that participants in a conversation enjoy being asked questions and tend to like the people asking questions more than those who answer them. But when third-party observers watch the same conversation unfold, they prefer the person who answers questions. This makes sense: People who mostly ask questions tend to disclose very little about themselves or their thoughts. To those listening to a conversation, question askers may come across as defensive, evasive, or invisible, while those answering seem more fascinating, present, or memorable.

The Best Response

A conversation is a dance that requires partners to be in sync—it's a mutual push-and-pull that unfolds over time. Just as the way we ask questions can facilitate trust and the sharing of information—so, too, can the way we answer them.

Answering questions requires making a choice about where to fall on a continuum between privacy and transparency. Should we answer the question? If we answer, how forthcoming should we be? What should we do when asked a question that, if answered truthfully, might reveal a less-than-glamorous fact or put us in a disadvantaged strategic position? Each end of the spectrum—fully opaque and fully transparent—has benefits and pitfalls. Keeping information private can make us feel free to experiment and learn. In negotiations, withholding sensitive information (such as the fact that your alternatives are weak) can help you secure better outcomes. At the same time, transparency is an essential part of forging meaningful connections. Even in a negotiation context, transparency can lead to value-creating deals; by sharing information, participants can identify elements that are relatively unimportant to one party but important to the other—the foundation of a win-win outcome.

And keeping secrets has costs. Research by Julie Lane and Daniel Wegner, of the University of Virginia, suggests that concealing secrets during social interactions leads to the intrusive recurrence of secret thoughts, while research by Columbia's

Michael Slepian, Jinseok Chun, and Malia Mason shows that keeping secrets—even outside of social interactions—depletes us cognitively, interferes with our ability to concentrate and remember things, and even harms long-term health and well-being.

In an organizational context, people too often err on the side of privacy—and underappreciate the benefits of transparency. How often do we realize that we could have truly bonded with a colleague only after he or she has moved on to a new company? Why are better deals often uncovered after the ink has dried, the tension has broken, and negotiators begin to chat freely?

To maximize the benefits of answering questions—and minimize the risks—it's important to decide before a conversation begins what information you want to share and what you want to keep private.

Deciding what to share

There is no rule of thumb for how much—or what type—of information you should disclose. Indeed, transparency is such a powerful bonding agent that sometimes it doesn't matter what is revealed—even information that reflects poorly on us can draw our conversational partners closer. In research Leslie conducted with HBS collaborators Kate Barasz and Michael Norton, she found that most people assume that it would be less damaging to refuse to answer a question that would reveal negative information—for example, "Have you ever been reprimanded at work?"—than to answer affirmatively. But this intuition is wrong. When they asked people to take the perspective of a recruiter and choose between two candidates (equivalent except for how they responded to this question), nearly 90% preferred the candidate who "came clean" and answered the question. Before a conversation takes place, think carefully about whether refusing to answer tough questions would do more harm than good.

Deciding what to keep private

Of course, at times you and your organization would be better served by keeping your cards close to your chest. In our negotiation classes, we teach strategies for handling hard questions without lying. Dodging, or answering a question you *wish* you had been asked, can be effective not only in helping you protect information you'd rather keep private but also in building a good rapport with your conversational partner, especially if you speak eloquently. In a study led by Todd Rogers, of Harvard's Kennedy School, participants were shown clips of political candidates responding to questions by either answering them or dodging them. Eloquent dodgers were liked more than ineloquent answerers, but only when their dodges went undetected. Another effective strategy is deflecting, or answering a probing question with another question or a joke. Answerers can use this approach to lead the conversation in a different direction.

. . .

"Question everything," Albert Einstein famously said. Personal creativity and organizational innovation rely on a willingness to seek out novel information. Questions and thoughtful answers foster smoother and more-effective interactions; they strengthen rapport and trust and lead groups toward discovery. All this we have documented in our research. But we believe questions and answers have a power that goes far beyond matters of performance. The wellspring of all questions is wonder and curiosity and a capacity for delight. We pose and respond to queries in the belief that the magic of a conversation will produce a whole that is greater than the sum of its parts. Sustained personal engagement and motivation—in our lives as well as our work—require that we are always mindful of the transformative joy of asking and answering questions.

Originally published in May–June 2018. Reprint R1803C

3

Taking the Stress Out of Stressful Conversations

by Holly Weeks

We live by talking. That's just the kind of animal we are. We chatter and tattle and gossip and jest. But sometimes—more often than we'd like—we have stressful conversations, those sensitive exchanges that can hurt or haunt us in ways no other kind of talking does. Stressful conversations are unavoidable in life, and in business they can run the gamut from firing a subordinate to, curiously enough, receiving praise. But whatever the context, stressful conversations differ from other conversations because of the emotional loads they carry. These conversations call up embarrassment, confusion, anxiety, anger, pain, or fear—if not in us, then in our counterparts. Indeed, stressful conversations cause such anxiety that most people simply avoid them. This strategy is not necessarily wrong. One of the first rules of engagement, after all, is to pick your battles. Yet sometimes it can be extremely costly to dodge issues, appease difficult people, and smooth over antagonisms because the fact is that avoidance usually makes a problem or relationship worse.

Since stressful conversations are so common—and so painful—why don't we work harder to improve them? The reason is precisely because our feelings are so enmeshed. When we are not emotionally entangled in an issue, we know that conflict is normal, that it can be resolved—or at least managed. But when feelings get stirred up, most of us are thrown off balance. Like a quarterback who chokes in a tight play, we lose all hope of ever making it to the goal line.

For the past 20 years, I have been teaching classes and conducting workshops at some of the top corporations and universities in the United States on how to communicate during stressful conversations. With classrooms as my laboratory, I have learned that most people feel incapable of talking through sensitive issues. It's as though all our skills go out the window and we can't think usefully about what's happening or what we could do to get good results.

Stressful conversations, though, need not be this way. I have seen that managers can improve difficult conversations unilaterally if they approach them with greater self-awareness, rehearse them in advance, and apply just three proven communication techniques. Don't misunderstand me: There will never be a cookie-cutter approach to stressful conversations. There are too many variables and too much tension, and the interactions between people in difficult situations are always unique. Yet nearly every stressful conversation can be seen as an amalgam of a limited number of basic conversations, each with its own distinct set of problems. In the following pages, we'll explore

Idea in Brief

Stressful conversations are unavoidable in life. In business, they can run the gamut from firing a subordinate to, curiously enough, receiving praise. But whatever the context, stressful conversations carry a heavy emotional load. Indeed, stressful conversations cause such anxiety that most people simply avoid them. Yet it can be extremely costly to dodge issues, appease difficult people, and smooth over antagonisms; avoidance usually only worsens a problem or a relationship. Using vivid examples of the three basic stressful conversations that people bump up against most often in the workplace, the author explains how managers can improve those interactions unilaterally. To begin with, they should approach the situations with greater self-awareness. Awareness building is not about endless self-analysis; much of it simply involves making tacit knowledge about oneself more explicit. Knowing how you react in a stressful situation will teach you a lot about your trouble areas and can help you master stressful situations. The author also recommends rehearsing difficult conversations in advance to fine-tune your phrasing and tone. We all know from past experience what kinds of conversations and people we handle badly. The trick is to have prepared conversational tactics to address those situations.

how you can anticipate and handle those problems. But first, let's look at the three basic stressful conversations that we bump up against most often in the workplace.

"I Have Bad News for You"

Delivering unpleasant news is usually difficult for both parties. The speaker is often tense, and the listener is apprehensive about where the conversation is headed. Consider David, the director of a nonprofit institution. He was in the uncomfortable position of needing to talk with an ambitious researcher, Jeremy, who had a much higher opinion of his job performance than others in the organization did. The complication for David was that, in the past,

Jeremy had received artificially high evaluations. There were several reasons for this. One had to do with the organization's culture: The nonprofit was not a confrontational kind of place. Additionally, Jeremy had tremendous confidence in both his own abilities and the quality of his academic background. Together with his defensive response to even the mildest criticism, this confidence led others—including David—to let slide discussions of weaknesses that were interfering with Jeremy's ability to deliver high-quality work. Jeremy had a cutting sense of humor, for instance, which had offended people inside and outside his unit. No one had ever said anything to him directly, but as time passed, more and more people were reluctant to work with him. Given that Jeremy had received almost no concrete criticism over the years, his biting style was now entrenched and the staff was restive.

In conversations like this, the main challenge is to get off to the right start. If the exchange starts off reasonably well, the rest of it has a good chance of going well. But if the opening goes badly, it threatens to bleed forward into the rest of the conversation. In an effort to be gentle, many people start these conversations on a light note. And that was just what David did, opening with, "How about those Red Sox?"

Naturally Jeremy got the wrong idea about where David was heading; he remained his usual cocky, superior self. Sensing this, David felt he had to take off the velvet gloves. The conversation quickly became brutally honest, and David did almost all the talking. When the monologue was over, Jeremy stared icily at the floor. He got up in stiff silence and left. David was relieved. From his point of view, the interaction had been painful but swift. There was not too much blood on the floor, he observed wryly. But two days later, Jeremy handed in his resignation, taking a lot of institutional memory—and talent—with him.

"What's Going On Here?"

Often we have stressful conversations thrust upon us. Indeed, some of the worst conversations—especially for people who are conflict averse—are the altogether unexpected ones that break out like crackling summer storms. Suddenly the conversation becomes intensely charged emotionally, and electricity flies in all directions. What's worse, nothing makes sense. We seem to have been drawn into a black cloud of twisted logic and altered sensibilities.

Consider the case of Elizabeth and Rafael. They were team leaders working together on a project for a major consulting firm. It seemed that everything that could have gone wrong on the project had, and the work was badly bogged down. The two consultants were meeting to revise their schedule, given the delays, and to divide up the discouraging tasks for the week ahead. As they talked, Elizabeth wrote and erased on the white board. When she had finished, she looked at Rafael and said matter-of-factly, "Is that it, then?"

Rafael clenched his teeth in frustration. "If you say so," he sniped.

Elizabeth recoiled. She instantly replayed the exchange in her mind but couldn't figure out what had provoked Rafael. His reaction seemed completely disconnected from her comment. The most common reaction of someone in Elizabeth's place is to guiltily defend herself by denying Rafael's unspoken accusation. But Elizabeth was uneasy with confrontation so she tried appeasement. "Rafael," she stammered, "I'm sorry. Is something wrong?"

"Who put you in charge?" he retorted. "Who told you to assign work to me?"

Clearly, Rafael and Elizabeth have just happened into a difficult conversation. Some transgression has occurred, but Elizabeth doesn't know exactly what it is. She feels blindsided—her attempt to expedite the task at hand has clearly been misconstrued. Rafael feels he's been put in a position of inferiority by what he sees as Elizabeth's controlling behavior. Inexplicably, there seem to be more than two people taking part in this conversation, and the invisible parties are creating lots of static. What childhood experience, we may wonder, is causing Elizabeth to assume that Rafael's tension is automatically her fault? And who is influencing Rafael's perception that Elizabeth is taking over? Could it be his father? His wife? It's impossible to tell. At the same time, it's hard for us to escape the feeling that Rafael is overreacting when he challenges Elizabeth about her alleged need to take control.

Elizabeth felt Rafael's resentment like a wave and she apologized again. "Sorry. How do you want the work divided?" Deferring to Rafael in this way smoothed the strained atmosphere for the time being. But it set a precedent for unequal status that neither Elizabeth nor the company believed was correct. Worse, though Rafael and Elizabeth remained on the same team after their painful exchange, Elizabeth chafed under the status change and three months later transferred out of the project.

"You Are Attacking Me!"

Now let's turn our attention to aggressively stressful conversations, those in which people use all kinds of psychological and rhetorical mechanisms to throw their counterparts off balance, to undermine their positions, even to expose and belittle them. These "thwarting tactics" take many forms—profanity, manipulation, shouting—and not everyone is triggered or stumped by the same ones. The red zone is not the thwarting tactic alone but the pairing of the thwarting tactic with individual vulnerability.

Consider Nick and Karen, two senior managers working at the same level in an IT firm. Karen was leading a presentation to a client, and the information was weak and disorganized. She and the team had not been able to answer even basic questions. The client had been patient, then quiet, then clearly exasperated. When the presentation really started to fall apart, the client put the team on the spot with questions that made them look increasingly inadequate.

On this particular day, Nick was not part of the presenting team; he was simply observing. He was as surprised as the client at Karen's poor performance. After the client left, he asked Karen what happened. She lashed out at him defensively: "You're not my boss, so don't start patronizing me. You always undercut me no matter what I do." Karen continued to shout at Nick, her antagonism palpable. Each time he spoke, she interrupted him with accusations and threats: "I can't wait to see how you like it when people leave you flailing in the wind." Nick tried to remain reasonable, but Karen didn't wind down. "Karen," he said, "pull yourself together. You are twisting every word I say."

Here, Nick's problem is not that Karen is using a panoply of thwarting tactics, but that all her tactics—accusation, distortion, and digression—are aggressive. This raises the stakes considerably. Most of us are vulnerable to aggressive tactics because we don't know whether, or how far, the aggression will escalate. Nick wanted to avoid Karen's aggression, but his insistence on rationality in the face of emotionalism was not working. His cool approach was trumped by Karen's aggressive one. As a result,

Nick found himself trapped in the snare of Karen's choosing. In particular, her threats that she would pay him back with the client rattled him. He couldn't tell whether she was just huffing or meant it. He finally turned to the managing director, who grew frustrated, and later angry, at Nick and Karen for their inability to resolve their problems. In the end, their lack of skill in handling their difficult conversations cost them dearly. Both were passed over for promotion after the company pinned the loss of the client directly on their persistent failure to communicate.

Preparing for a Stressful Conversation

So how can we prepare for these three basic stressful conversations before they occur? A good start is to become aware of your own weaknesses to people and situations. David, Elizabeth, and Nick were unable to control their counterparts, but their stressful conversations would have gone much better if they had been more usefully aware of their vulnerabilities. It is important for those who are vulnerable to hostility, for example, to know how they react to it. Do they withdraw or escalate—do they clam up or retaliate? While one reaction is not better than the other, knowing how you react in a stressful situation will teach you a lot about your vulnerabilities, and it can help you master stressful situations.

Recall Nick's problem. If he had been more self-aware, he would have known that he acts stubbornly rational in the face of aggressive outbursts such as Karen's. Nick's choice of a disengaged demeanor gave Karen control over the conversation, but he didn't have to allow Karen—or anyone else—to exploit his vulnerability. In moments of calm self-scrutiny, when he's not entangled in a live stressful conversation, Nick can take time to reflect on his inability to tolerate irrational aggressive outbursts. This self-awareness would free him to prepare himself—not for Karen's unexpected accusations but for his own predictable vulnerability to any sudden assault like hers.

Though it might sound like it, building awareness is not about endless self-analysis. Much of it simply involves making our tacit knowledge about ourselves more explicit. We all know from past experience, for instance, what kinds of conversations and people we handle badly. When you find yourself in a difficult conversation, ask yourself whether this is one of those situations and whether it involves one of those people. For instance, do you bare your teeth when faced with an overbearing competitor? Do you shut down when you feel excluded? Once you know what your danger zones are, you can anticipate your vulnerability and improve your response.

Explicit self-awareness will often help save you from engaging in a conversation in a way that panders to your feelings rather than one that serves your needs. Think back to David, the boss of the nonprofit institution, and Jeremy, his cocky subordinate. Given Jeremy's history, David's conversational game plan—easing in, then when that didn't work, the painful-but-quick bombshell—was doomed. A better approach would have been for David to split the conversation into two parts. In a first meeting, he could have raised the central issues of Jeremy's biting humor and disappointing performance. A second meeting could have been set up for the discussion itself. Handling the situation incrementally would have allowed time for both David and Jeremy to prepare for a two-way conversation instead of one of them delivering a monologue. After all, this wasn't an emergency; David didn't have to exhaust this topic immediately. Indeed, if David had been more self-aware, he

The DNA of Conversation Management

The techniques I have identified for handling stressful conversations all have tucked within them three deceptively simple ingredients that are needed to make stressful conversations succeed. These are clarity, neutrality, and temperance, and they are the building blocks of all good communication. Mastering them will multiply your chances of responding well to even the most strained conversation. Let's take a look at each of the components in turn.

Clarity means letting words do the work for us. Avoid euphemisms or talking in circles—tell people clearly what you mean: "Emily, from your family's point of view, the Somerset Valley Nursing Home would be the best placement for your father. His benefits don't cover it." Unfortunately, delivering clear content when the news is bad is particularly hard to do. Under strained circumstances, we all tend to shy away from clarity because we equate it with brutality. Instead, we often say things like: "Well, Dan, we're still not sure yet what's going to happen with this job, but in the future we'll keep our eyes open." This is a roundabout—and terribly misleading—way to inform someone that he didn't get the promotion he was seeking. Yet there's nothing inherently brutal about honesty. It is not the content but the delivery of the news that makes it brutal or humane. Ask a surgeon; ask a priest; ask a cop. If a message is given skillfully—even though the news is bad—the content may still be tolerable. When a senior executive, for example, directly tells a subordinate that "the promotion has gone to someone else," the news is likely to be highly unpleasant,

might have recognized that the approach he chose was dictated less by Jeremy's character than by his own distaste for conflict.

An excellent way to anticipate specific problems that you may encounter in a stressful conversation is to rehearse with a neutral friend. Pick someone who doesn't have the same communication and the appropriate reaction is sadness, anger, and anxiety. But if the content is clear, the listener can better begin to process the information. Indeed, bringing clarity to the content eases the burden for the counterpart rather than increasing it.

Tone is the nonverbal part of delivery in stressful conversations. It is intonation, facial expressions, conscious and unconscious body language. Although it's hard to have a neutral tone when overcome by strong feelings, neutrality is the desired norm in crisis communications, including stressful conversations. Consider the classic neutrality of NASA. Regardless of how dire the message, NASA communicates its content in uninflected tones: "Houston, we have a problem." It takes practice to acquire such neutrality. But a neutral tone is the best place to start when a conversation turns stressful.

Temperate phrasing is the final element in this triumvirate of skills. English is a huge language, and there are lots of different ways to say what you need to say. Some of these phrases are temperate, while others baldly provoke your counterpart to dismiss your words—and your content. In the United States, for example, some of the most intemperate phrasing revolves around threats of litigation: "If you don't get a check to me by April 23, I'll be forced to call my lawyer." Phrases like this turn up the heat in all conversations, particularly in strained ones. But remember, we're not in stressful conversations to score points or to create enemies. The goal is to advance the conversation, to hear and be heard accurately, and to have a functional exchange between two people. So next time you want to snap at someone—"Stop interrupting me!"—try this: "Can you hold on a minute? I want to finish before I lose my train of thought." Temperate phrasing will help you take the strain out of a stressful conversation.

problems as you. Ideally, the friend should be a good listener, honest but nonjudgmental. Start with content. Just tell your friend what you want to say to your counterpart without worrying about tone or phrasing. Be vicious, be timid, be sarcastically witty, jump around in your argument, but get it out. Now go over it again and think about what you would say if the situation weren't emotionally loaded. Your friend can help you because he or she is not in a flush of emotion over the situation. Write down what you come up with together because if you don't, you'll forget it later.

Now fine-tune the phrasing. When you imagine talking to the counterpart, your phrasing tends to be highly charged—and you can think of only one way to say anything. But when your friend says, "Tell me how you want to say this," an interesting thing happens: Your phrasing is often much better, much more temperate, usable. Remember, you can say what you want to say, you just can't say it *like that*. Also, work on your body language with your friend. You'll both soon be laughing because of the expressions that sneak out unawares—eyebrows skittering up and down, legs wrapped around each other like licorice twists, nervous snickers that will certainly be misinterpreted. (For more on preparing for stressful conversations, see the sidebar "The DNA of Conversation Management.")

Managing the Conversation

While it is important to build awareness and to practice before a stressful conversation, these steps are not enough. Let's look at what you can do as the conversation unfolds. Consider Elizabeth, the team leader whose colleague claimed she was usurping control. She couldn't think well on her feet in confrontational situations, and she knew it, so she needed a few hip-pocket phrases—phrases she could recall on the spot so that she wouldn't have to be silent or invent something on the spur of the moment. Though such a solution sounds simple, most of us don't have a tool kit of conversational tactics ready at hand. Rectifying this gap is an essential part of learning how to handle stressful conversations better. We need to learn communications skills, in the same way that we learn CPR: well in advance, knowing that when we need to use them, the situation will be critical and tense. Here are three proven conversational gambits. The particular wording may not suit your style, and that's fine. The important thing is to understand how the techniques work, and then choose phrasing that is comfortable for you.

Honor thy partner

When David gave negative feedback to Jeremy, it would have been refreshing if he had begun with an admission of regret and some responsibility for his contribution to their shared problem. "Jeremy," he might have said, "the quality of your work has been undercut—in part by the reluctance of your colleagues to risk the edge of your humor by talking problems through with you. I share responsibility for this because I have been reluctant to speak openly about these difficulties with you, whom I like and respect and with whom I have worked a long time." Acknowledging responsibility as a technique—particularly as an opening—can be effective because it immediately focuses attention, but without provocation, on the difficult things the speaker needs to say and the listener needs to hear.

Is this always a good technique in a difficult conversation? No, because there is never any one good technique. But in this case, it effectively sets the tone for David's discussion with Jeremy. It honors the problems, it honors Jeremy, it honors their relationship, and it honors David's responsibility. Any technique that communicates honor in a stressful conversation—particularly a conversation that will take the counterpart by surprise—is to be highly valued. Indeed, the ability to act with dignity can make or break a stressful conversation. More important, while Jeremy has left the company, he can still do harm by spreading gossip and using his insider's knowledge against the organization. The more intolerable the conversation with David has been, the more Jeremy is likely to make the organization pay.

Disarm by restating your intentions

Part of the difficulty in Rafael and Elizabeth's "What's Going On Here?" conversation is that Rafael's misinterpretation of Elizabeth's words and actions seems to be influenced by instant replays of other stressful conversations that he has had in the past. Elizabeth doesn't want to psychoanalyze Rafael; indeed, exploring Rafael's internal landscape would exacerbate this painful situation. So what can Elizabeth do to defuse the situation unilaterally?

Elizabeth needs a technique that doesn't require her to understand the underlying reasons for Rafael's strong reaction but helps her handle the situation effectively. "I can see how you took what I said the way you did, Rafael. That wasn't what I meant. Let's go over this list again." I call this the clarification technique, and it's a highly disarming one. Using it, Elizabeth can unilaterally change the confrontation into a point of agreement. Instead of arguing with Rafael about his perceptions, she grants him his perceptions—after all, they're his. Instead of arguing about her intentions, she keeps the responsibility for aligning her words with her intentions on her side. And she goes back into the conversation right where they left off. (For a fuller discussion of the disconnect between what we mean and what we say, see the sidebar "The Gap Between Communication and Intent.")

This technique will work for Elizabeth regardless of Rafael's motive. If Rafael innocently misunderstood what she was saying, she isn't fighting him. She accepts his take on what she said and did and corrects it. If his motive is hostile, Elizabeth doesn't concur

The Gap Between Communication and Intent

One of the most common occurrences in stressful conversations is that we all start relying far too much on our intentions. As the mercury in the emotional thermometer rises, we presume that other people automatically understand what we mean. We assume, for instance, that people know we mean well. Indeed, research shows that in stressful conversations, most speakers assume that the listener believes that they have good intentions, regardless of what they say. Intentions can never be that powerful in communications—and certainly not in stressful conversations.

To see what I mean, just think of the last time someone told you not to take something the wrong way. This may well have been uttered quite sincerely by the speaker; nevertheless, most people automatically react by stiffening inwardly, anticipating something at least mildly offensive or antagonistic. And that is exactly the reaction that phrase is always going to get. Because the simplest rule about stressful conversations is that people don't register intention despite words; we register intention through words. In stressful conversations in particular, the emphasis is on what is actually said, not on what we intend or feel. This doesn't mean that participants in stressful conversations don't have feelings or intentions that are valid and valuable. They do. But when we talk about people in stressful communication, we're talking about communication between people—and not about intentions.

Of course, in difficult conversations we may all wish that we didn't have to be so explicit. We may want the other person to realize what we mean even if we don't spell it out. But that leads to the wrong division of labor—with the listener interpreting rather than the speaker communicating. In all conversations, but especially in stressful ones, we are all responsible for getting across to one another precisely what we want to say. In the end, it's far more dignified for an executive to come right out and tell an employee: "Corey, I've arranged a desk for you—and six weeks of outplacement service—because you won't be with us after the end of July." Forcing someone to guess your intentions only prolongs the agony of the inevitable.

just to appease him. She accepts and retries. No one loses face. No one scores points off the other. No one gets drawn off on a tangent.

Fight tactics, not people

Rafael may have baffled Elizabeth, but Karen was acting with outright malice toward Nick when she flew off the handle after a disastrous meeting with the client. Nick certainly can't prevent her from using the thwarting tactics with which she has been so successful in the past. But he can separate Karen's character from her behavior. For instance, it's much more useful for him to think of Karen's reactions as thwarting tactics rather than as personal characteristics. If he thinks of Karen as a distorting, hostile, threatening person, where does that lead? What can anyone ever do about another person's character? But if Nick sees Karen's behavior as a series of tactics that she is using with him because they have worked for her in the past, he can think about using countering techniques to neutralize them.

The best way to neutralize a tactic is to name it. It's much harder to use a tactic once it is openly identified. If Nick, for instance, had said, "Karen, we've worked together pretty well for a long time. I don't know how to talk about what went wrong in the meeting when your take on what happened, and what's going on now, is so different from mine," he would have changed the game completely. He neither would have attacked Karen nor remained the pawn of her tactics. But he would have made Karen's tactics in the conversation the dominant problem.

Openly identifying a tactic, particularly an aggressive one, is disarming for another reason. Often we think of an aggressive counterpart as persistently, even endlessly, contentious, but that isn't true. People have definite levels of aggression that they're comfortable with—and they are reluctant to raise the bar. When Nick doesn't acknowledge Karen's tactics, she can use them unwittingly, or allegedly so. But if Nick speaks of them, it would require more aggression on Karen's part to continue using the same tactics. If she is at or near her aggression threshold, she won't continue because that would make her uncomfortable. Nick may not be able to stop Karen, but she may stop herself.

People think stressful conversations are inevitable. And they are. But that doesn't mean they have to have bad resolutions. Consider a client of mine, Jacqueline, the only woman on the board of an engineering company. She was sensitive to slighting remarks about women in business, and she found one board member deliberately insensitive. He repeatedly ribbed her about being a feminist and, on this occasion, he was telling a sexist joke.

This wasn't the first time that something like this had happened, and Jacqueline felt the usual internal cacophony of reactions. But because she was aware that this was a stressful situation for her, Jacqueline was prepared. First, she let the joke hang in the air for a minute and then went back to the issue they had been discussing. When Richard didn't let it go but escalated with a new poke—"Come on, Jackie, it was a *joke*"—Jacqueline stood her ground. "Richard," she said, "this kind of humor is frivolous to you, but it makes me feel pushed aside." Jacqueline didn't need to say more. If Richard had continued to escalate, he would have lost face. In fact, he backed down: "Well, I wouldn't want my wife to hear about my bad behavior a second time," he snickered. Jacqueline was silent. She had made her point; there was no need to embarrass him.

Stressful conversations are never easy, but we can all fare better if, like Jacqueline, we prepare for them by developing greater awareness of our vulnerabilities and better techniques for handling ourselves. The advice and tools described in this article can be helpful in unilaterally reducing the strain in stressful conversations. All you have to do is try them. If one technique doesn't work, try another. Find phrasing that feels natural. But keep practicing—you'll find what works best for you.

Originally published in July–August 2001. Reprint R0107H

How Supportive Leaders Approach Emotional Conversations

by Sarah Noll Wilson

The emotional strain of modern life has made it increasingly clear that managers need to shift their focus to meeting and supporting employees' emotional well-being. It's no longer enough to simply provide the operational tools and resources for your team to function—you also need to create psychological safety for them to thrive. That means getting comfortable with having uncomfortable conversations.

It can be hard to know the right thing to say when someone discloses something painful or emotional to you. For example, one of our clients, Evie (not her real name), an IT manager, suffered through a miscarriage while working from home a few years ago. Her boss, Mike, could tell something was off and called her to check in. She didn't want to lie, so she took a deep, courageous breath and shared, "You know, to be completely transparent with you, I want to let you know I am coping with a recent miscarriage and really struggling with that . . . mentally and physically." Mike was silent for a while before finally saying, "Well . . . do what you need to do," and then ending the phone call. Mike's reaction has stuck with Evie to this day, years later. In a moment of loss and suffering, she felt entirely unsupported. Was this his intention? No, but it was his impact.

As leaders, it's imperative that we take the time to learn how to show up for our employees, no matter how uncomfortable the situations they face may be for us. For productivity and innovation to thrive, we need to create environments where the team members we serve can thrive. Kelly Greenwood and Julia Anas, who surveyed 1,500 U.S. adults in full-time jobs, outline the benefits of supporting employee mental health in their article, "It's a New Era for Mental Health at Work." They write:

> *Respondents who felt supported by their employer also tended to be less likely to experience mental health symptoms, less likely to underperform and miss work, and more likely to feel comfortable talking about their mental health at work. In addition, they had higher job satisfaction and intentions to stay at their company. Lastly, they had more positive views of their company and its leaders, including trusting their company and being proud to work there.*

We heard from a client that their leaders had been asking them how they were doing more often, but it was clear that the leaders didn't know how to respond to the answers, which ranged from "OK" to "struggling" to "drowning" and beyond. Checking

Idea in Brief

The Problem

Many leaders aren't aware when they're using emotionally dismissive and potentially harmful language with their employees. Most of the time, it comes from a place of caring, but, in an attempt to minimize pain, a leader may leave the employee feeling minimized instead. On the other hand, some leaders believe that emotions don't belong in the workplace at all.

The Reality

Emotional strain is a fact of modern life. It's no longer enough for managers to simply provide the operational tools and resources their team needs to function—they also need to create psychological safety for team members to thrive.

The Solution

That means getting comfortable with having uncomfortable conversations. The author presents six ways for managers to be supportive when someone shares an emotional situation or challenge.

in is an important first step, but how you react to what's shared creates the ultimate impact. Using emotionally supportive language is a vital part of that.

What Emotionally Dismissive Language Sounds Like

Many leaders aren't aware when they're using emotionally dismissive and potentially harmful language with their employees. In our experience with hundreds of leaders, unintentionally dismissive language often comes from a place of caring. They want to support the person, help them move through their issue, and minimize their pain. But sometimes, in an attempt to minimize the pain, they minimize the person as well.

On the other hand, some leaders believe that emotions don't belong in the workplace. This lack of empathy can prevent them from understanding who the person is and what they're going through. They ignore the reality that emotions inform decision-making and problem-solving, and they fail to harness the opportunities for growth that emotions can create. Ignoring emotions doesn't make them go away.

Let's look at a few common scenarios that come up when people share mental and emotional struggles:

- *Dismissive phrasing,* such as "What do you have to be sad about?" or "You shouldn't be sad—you have an excellent job/family/etc."

- *Minimization,* which can be anything from "Everyone feels like that sometimes" to "There's nothing to worry about."

- *Negation,* which usually sounds like "Hey, it could be worse!" or "That's just a 'first-world problem.'"

- *Prescribing solutions,* like saying "You shouldn't worry" or "You just need to get more sleep."

- *Toxic positivity,* which may sound like "Just look at the bright side!" or "Everything happens for a reason!" A positive perspective can be helpful but can become unproductive when it's the only perspective offered.

Using dismissive language in these ways can send a message to the recipient that their feelings and struggles aren't real or are unnecessary—and it can even amplify any shame that's already present. If someone is coming to you because they're struggling, the last thing you want is for them to leave feeling unseen, unheard, and unsupported.

What Emotionally Supportive Language Sounds Like

Becoming a more emotionally supportive leader requires emotional intelligence. Farah Harris, well-being expert and founder of WorkingWell Daily, described emotionally intelligent leaders to me as "comfortable with emotions—whether those that come up within them or come up in others. They create a sense of belonging because their behaviors allow their team members to be seen and heard."

Emotionally intelligent leaders don't hide behind a shield of detachment when someone presents them with a struggle. They can regulate their own emotions and support others in doing the same.

Here are six ways to be supportive when someone shares an emotional situation or challenge.

Validate their experience

Validation can be as simple as acknowledgment—for example, "I can see why this is exhausting." Especially when experiencing mental health challenges, people can feel alone and even broken. By validating someone's experience, you're not only saying "I see you," you're also saying "I believe you"—which can bring comfort during a challenging time.

Seek to understand

Give your team member the opportunity to elaborate if they want to. Coming from a place of curiosity can be powerful—for example, "Tell me more about that." When we seek to understand, we show the other person that we care about them, want to support them, and want to learn more so we can do more.

Guide emotional and physical support

When someone is struggling, you might ask, "How can I best support you right now?" or "What would be helpful?" In a heightened emotional moment, it can be hard for someone to think about or identify what may help them. Asking this question can prompt them to pause, reflect, and name what they need.

Offer specific support

Sometimes people don't know what they need, may be afraid to ask, or are unsure of what options are available. You might ask, "Would X be helpful?" Offering a concrete suggestion can make it easier for someone to accept help.

Invite perspective instead of prescribing a solution

If you've been through a similar experience as your team member, don't assume you fully understand or that what worked for you will work for them. Knowing that someone has faced something similar can be comforting, but everyone is on a different journey. Assuming you know what's best can minimize the other person's needs, center the conversation on you, and leave them feeling unsupported. Instead of saying "I've been there—here's what you should do," try "Would it be helpful to hear what helped me in a similar situation?"

Acknowledge and appreciate them

Thank your team member for coming to you—for example: "I can see this has been hard. I'm here for you. Thank you for trusting me with this information." This signals to both you and them that conversations like this are important, and reinforces a sense of safety for future situations.

Emotional Supportiveness in Action

As leaders, we often want to help soothe and remove discomfort. If we're honest, there are also times when we want to remove the discomfort not just for our team members but for ourselves as well. It's not our job to heal them, but to make it safe for them to share and to provide whatever support we can. It's OK if you don't know what to say—in fact, simply acknowledging that can be powerful, too.

In 2013, I was diagnosed with panic disorder, which meant I was experiencing repeated episodes of panic attacks. I was new to my company at the time and desperately tried to hide this new challenge and quickly clean up any residual tears before meetings. My company's CHRO pulled me aside and asked me how I was doing. After a pause, she then asked, "How are you really doing?" I stood at the edge of her door so I could escape if I needed, biting my lip and nervous to share. But I started to talk—and the tears flowed. She listened, validated how scary this must have been for me, and reassured me that the company would support me in whatever way I needed. Finally, she thanked me for sharing. At a time when everything felt heavy, work unexpectedly became a place where things felt a little lighter.

As we continue into new chapters of navigating political turmoil, racial injustice, divisiveness, and constant uncertainty, do you want to be the leader who adds to the weight—or the one who makes it a little lighter? Learning how to have uncomfortable conversations can help ensure that you're setting up your team members to thrive.

Adapted from hbr.org, March 1, 2022. Reprint H06VSM

4

The Science of Strong Business Writing

by Bill Birchard

S trong writing skills are essential for anyone in business. You need them to effectively communicate with colleagues, employees, and bosses and to sell any ideas, products, or services you're offering.

Many people, especially in the corporate world, think good writing is an art—and that those who do it well have an innate talent they've nurtured through experience, intuition, and a habit of reading often and widely. But every day we're learning more about the science of good writing. Advances in neurobiology and psychology show, with data and in images, exactly how the brain responds to words, phrases, and stories. And the criteria for making better writing choices are more objective than you might think.

Good writing gets the reader's dopamine flowing in the area of the brain known as the reward circuit. Great writing releases opioids that turn on reward hot spots. Just like good food, a soothing bath, or an enveloping hug, well-executed prose makes us feel pleasure, which makes us want to keep reading.

Most of the rules you learned in school—"Show, don't tell" or "Use the active voice"—still hold. But the reasons they do are now clearer. Scientists using MRI and PET machines can literally see how reward regions clustered in the midbrain light up when people read certain types of writing or hear it spoken aloud. Each word, phrase, or idea acts as a stimulus, causing the brain to instantly answer a stream of questions: Does this promise value? Will I like it? Can I learn from it?

Kent Berridge, a pioneering University of Michigan psychologist and neuroscientist, notes that researchers originally believed that the reward circuit largely handled sensory cues. But, he explains, "it's become clear in the past 50 years from neuroimaging studies that all kinds of social and cultural rewards can also activate this system."

Whether it's a succinct declarative statement in an email or a complex argument in a report, your own writing has the potential to light up the neural circuitry of your readers' brains. (The same is true if you read the words to an audience.) The magic happens when prose has one or more of these characteristics: It's simple, specific, surprising, stirring, seductive, smart, social, or story-driven. In my work as an author and a writing coach for businesspeople, I've found those eight S's to be hallmarks of the best writing. And scientific evidence backs up their power.

Simplicity

"Keep it simple." This classic piece of writing advice stands on the most basic neuroscience research. Simplicity increases what scientists call the brain's "processing fluency." Short sentences,

Idea in Brief

The Research

Brain scans are showing us in new detail exactly what entices readers. Scientists can see a group of midbrain neurons—the "reward circuit"—light up as people respond to everything from a simple metaphor to an unexpected story twist. The big takeaway? Whether you're crafting an email to a colleague or an important report for the board, you can write in a way that delights readers on a primal level, releasing pleasure chemicals in their brains.

How to Do It

There are eight features of satisfying writing: simplicity, specificity, surprise, stirring language, seductiveness, smart ideas, social content, and storytelling. They're effective tools for engaging readers because they trigger the same neural responses that other pleasurable stimuli do. Learning how to use these eight S's can captivate readers and help your message stick.

familiar words, and clean syntax ensure that the reader doesn't have to exert too much brainpower to understand your meaning.

By contrast, studies have shown that sentences with clauses nested in the middle take longer to read and cause more comprehension mistakes. Ditto for most sentences in the passive voice. If you write "Profits are loved by investors," for example, instead of "Investors love profits," you're switching the standard positions of the verb and the direct object. That can cut comprehension accuracy by 10% and take a tenth of a second longer to read.

Tsuyoshi Okuhara, of the University of Tokyo, teamed with colleagues to ask 400 people aged 40 to 69 to read about how to exercise for better health. Half the group got long-winded, somewhat technical material. The other half got an easy-to-read edit of the same content. The group reading the simple version—with shorter words and sentences, among other things—scored higher on self-efficacy: They expressed more confidence in succeeding.

Even more noteworthy: Humans learn from experience that simpler explanations are not always right, but they *usually* are. Andrey Kolmogorov, a Russian mathematician, proved decades ago that people infer that simpler patterns yield better predictions, explanations, and decisions. That means you're more persuasive when you reduce overdressed ideas to their naked state.

Cutting extraneous words and using the active voice are two ways to keep it simple. Another tactic is to drill down to what's really salient and scrap tangential details. Let's say you have researched crossover markets and are recommending options in a memo to senior leaders. Instead of sharing every pro and con for each market—that is, taking the exhaustive approach— maybe pitch just the top two prospects and identify their principal pluses and minuses.

Specificity

Specifics awaken a swath of brain circuits. Think of "pelican" versus "bird." Or "wipe" versus "clean." In one study, the more-specific words in those pairs activated more neurons in the visual and motor-strip parts of the brain than did the general ones, which means they caused the brain to process meaning more robustly.

Years ago scientists thought our brains decoded words as symbols. Now we understand that our neurons actually "embody" what the words mean: When we hear more-specific ones, we "taste," "feel," and "see" traces of the real thing.

Remarkably, the simulation may extend to our muscles too. When a team led by an Italian researcher, Marco Tettamanti, asked people to listen to sentences related to the mouth, hand,

and leg—"I bite an apple"; "I grasp a knife"; "I kick the ball"—the brain regions for moving their jaws, hands, and legs fired.

Using more-vivid, palpable language will reward your readers. In a recent letter to shareholders, Amazon CEO Jeff Bezos didn't say, "We're facing strong competition." Channeling Tettamanti's research, he wrote, "Third-party sellers are kicking our first-party butt. Badly."

Another specificity tactic is to give readers a memorable shorthand phrase to help them retain your message. Malcolm Gladwell coined "the tipping point." Management gurus W. Chan Kim and Renée Mauborgne came up with "blue ocean strategy"; essayist Nassim Nicholas Taleb, "black swan event."

Surprise

Our brains are wired to make nonstop predictions, including guessing the next word in every line of text. If your writing confirms the readers' guess, that's OK, though possibly a yawner. Surprise can make your message stick, helping readers learn and retain information.

Jean-Louis Dessalles, a researcher in artificial intelligence and cognitive science at Télécom Paris, conducted an experiment that demonstrated people's affinity for the unexpected. He asked participants to read short, unfinished narratives and consider different possible endings for each. For example, one story read: "Two weeks after my car had been stolen, the police informed me that a car that might be mine was for sale on the internet. . . . The phone number had been identified. It was the mobile phone number of. . . ." The choices were (a) "my office colleague," (b) "a colleague of my brother's," or (c) "someone in my neighborhood." For 17 of 18 stories, the vast majority of people preferred the most unexpected ending (in this example, the work colleague). They didn't want a story that fulfilled their predictions.

So reward your readers with novelty. Jonah Berger and Katherine Milkman, of the Wharton School, saw the impact of surprising content when they examined nearly 7,000 articles that appeared online in the *New York Times*. They found that those rated as surprising were 14% more likely to be on the newspaper's "most-emailed" list.

Readers appreciate unusual wordplay, too. A good example is John McPhee's characterization of World War II as a "technological piñata." Or consider how a Texas-based conglomerate described itself in its 2016 shareholder letter: "Think of Biglari Holdings as a museum of businesses. Our preference is to collect masterpieces."

Stirring Language

You may think you're more likely to persuade with logic, but no. Our brains process the emotional connotations of a word within 200 milliseconds of reading it—much faster than we understand its meaning. So when we read emotionally charged material, we reflexively react with feelings—fear, joy, awe, disgust, and so forth—because our brains have been trained since hunter-gatherer times to respond that way. Reason follows. We then combine the immediate feeling and subsequent thought to create meaning.

How sensitive are we to emotion? Experiments show that when people hear a list of words, they often miss a few as a result of "attentional blinks" caused by limits in our brain processing power. But we don't miss the emotionally significant words. With those there are no blinks.

So when you write your next memo, consider injecting words that package feeling and thought together. Instead of saying "challenge the competition," you might use "outwit rivals." In lieu of "promote innovation," try "prize ingenuity." Metaphor often works even better. Canadian researchers Andrea Bowes and Albert Katz tested relatively bland phrases like "What a very good idea!" and "Be careful what you say" against more-evocative expressions like "What a gem of an idea!" and "Watch your back." Readers reacted more strongly to the latter.

Just a small touch can drive the neural circuits for emotion. So before you start composing, get your feelings straight, along with your facts. Zeal for your message will show through. And if you express your emotion, readers will feel it.

Seductiveness

As humans, we're wired to savor anticipation. One famous study showed that people are often happier planning a vacation than they are after taking one. Scientists call the reward "anticipatory utility." You can build up the same sort of excitement when you structure your writing. In experiments using poetry, researchers found that readers' reward circuitry reached peak firing several seconds before the high points of emphatic lines and stanzas. Brain images show preemptive spikes of pleasure even in readers with no previous interest in poetry.

You can generate a similar reaction by winding up people's curiosity for what's to come. Steve Jobs did this in his famous "How to Live Before You Die" commencement address to Stanford University's class of 2005. "I never graduated from college," he began. "Truth be told, this is the closest I've ever gotten to a college graduation. Today I want to tell you three stories from my life. That's it. No big deal. Just three stories." Are you on the edge of your seat to hear what the three stories are?

So start a report with a question. Pose your customer problem as a conundrum. Position your product development work as solving a mystery. Put readers in a state of uncertainty so that you can then lead them to something better.

Smart Thinking

Making people feel smart—giving them an "aha" moment—is another way to please readers. To show how these sudden "pops" of insight activate the brain, researchers have asked people to read three words (for example, "house," "bark," and "apple") and then identify a fourth word that relates to all three, while MRI machines and EEGs record their brain activity. When the study participants arrive at a solution ("tree"), brain regions near the right temple light up, and so do parts of the reward circuit in the prefrontal cortex and midbrain. The readers' delight is visible. Psychological research also reveals how people feel after such moments: at ease, certain, and—most of all—happy.

How can you write to create an aha moment for your readers? One way is to draw fresh distinctions. Ginni Rometty, formerly IBM's CEO, offered one with this description of the future: "It will not be a world of man versus machine; it will be a world of man plus machine."

Another strategy is to phrase a pragmatic message so that it also evokes a perennial, universal truth. The late Max De Pree, founder and CEO of the office furniture company Herman Miller, had a knack for speaking to employees this way. In *Leadership Is an Art* he wrote: "The first responsibility of a leader is to define reality. The last is to say thank you. In between the two, the leader must become a servant and a debtor." That's wisdom not just for business managers but for parents, teachers, coaches—anyone in a guiding role.

Social Content

Our brains are wired to crave human connection—even in what we read. Consider a study of readers' responses to different kinds of literary excerpts, some with vivid descriptions of people or their thoughts, and others without such a focus. The passages that included people activated the areas of participants' brains that interpret social signals, which in turn triggered their reward circuits.

We don't want just to read about people, though—we want to understand what they're thinking as quickly as possible. A study led by Frank Van Overwalle, a social neuroscientist at Vrije Universiteit Brussel, found that readers infer the goals of people they're reading about in under 350 milliseconds, and discern their character traits within 650 milliseconds.

One way to help readers connect with you and your writing is to reveal more traces of yourself in it. Think voice, worldview, vocabulary, wit, syntax, poetic rhythm, sensibilities. Take the folksy—and effective—speeches and letters of Berkshire Hathaway CEO Warren Buffett. His bon mots include "Someone's sitting in the shade today because someone planted a tree a long time ago," "It's only when the tide goes out that you discover who's been swimming naked," and "Beware of geeks bearing formulas."

Remember also to include the human angle in any topic you're discussing. When you want to make a point about a supply-chain hiccup, for example, don't frame the problem as a "trucking disconnect." Write instead about mixed signals between the driver and dispatcher.

Another simple trick to engage readers is to use the second person ("you"), as I've done throughout this piece. This can be particularly helpful when you're explaining technical or complicated material. For example, psychologist Richard Mayer and colleagues at the University of California, Santa Barbara, ran experiments with two versions of an online presentation on the respiratory system. Each included 100 words of spoken text paired with simple animations. But one version used the impersonal third person ("During inhaling, *the* diaphragm moves down, creating more space for *the* lungs . . ."), while the other was more personal ("*your* diaphragm" and "*your* lungs"). People who listened to the latter scored significantly higher than their counterparts on a test that measured what they had learned.

Storytelling

Few things beat a good anecdote. Stories, even fragments of them, captivate extensive portions of readers' brains in part because they combine many of the elements I've described already.

Research by Uri Hasson at Princeton reveals the neural effect of an engaging tale. Functional MRI scans show that when a story begins, listeners' brains immediately begin glowing in a specific pattern. What's more, that grid reflects the storyteller's exactly. Other research shows that, at the same time, midbrain regions of the reward circuit come to life.

Experiments by behavioral scientists at the University of Florida produced similar results. Brain images showed heightened activity in reward regions among people who read 12-second narratives that prompted pleasant images. (A sample narrative: "It's the last few minutes of the big game and it's close. The crowd explodes in a deafening roar. You jump up, cheering. Your team has come from behind to win.")

When you incorporate stories into your communications, big payoffs can result. Consider research that Melissa Lynne Murphy did at the University of Texas, looking at business crowdfunding campaigns. She found that study participants formed more-favorable impressions of the pitches that had richer narratives, giving them higher marks for entrepreneur credibility and business legitimacy. Study participants also expressed more willingness to invest in the projects and share information about them. The implication: No stories, no great funding success.

. . .

The eight S's can be your secret weapons in writing well. They're effective tools for engaging readers because they trigger the same neural responses that other pleasurable stimuli do. And you probably understand their value intuitively because millions of years of evolution have trained our brains to know what feels right. So cultivate those instincts. They'll lead you to the writer's version of the Golden Rule: Reward readers as you would yourself.

Originally published in July–August 2021. Reprint R2104L

Did You Get My Slack/Email/Text?

by Erica Dhawan

Before remote working became prevalent, we all knew the unwritten rules of communication in the office. If someone had headphones on, they were probably focused on work and didn't want to be interrupted to gossip about the latest drama. Or, if your team was about to have an important meeting with a client, you would quickly run through last-minute questions before walking into the room.

We all learned these communication norms by observing our colleagues. But now, with the shift to hybrid work, there is a need to create new rules for digital communication. Somehow, it seems that the more platforms we have at our disposal, the more complicated digital communication gets.

In 2021, I published a research study with Quester called *The Digital Communication Crisis* to understand the challenges we all face in workplace digital communication. Through a survey of almost 2,000 office workers, we found that more than 70% had experienced some form of unclear communication from their colleagues. This leads to the average employee wasting four hours per week on poor or confusing digital communication, which adds up to an average of $188 billion wasted annually across the American economy.[1]

Here's an example of one organization that was struggling with this very issue. The organization brought me in to assess a team's digital communication channels. The division leader wanted to know why there was so much daily dysfunction: missed deadlines, ignored emails, reports of uncomfortable chat room conversations, and a lot of peer-based passive-aggressiveness.

It didn't take me long to discover that the team in question was using its collaboration tools in every way but the right one. In their hands, Microsoft Teams chat had become a devious way for members to avoid video-call collaboration. Members were also sharing the same messages and documents across multiple collaboration tools, making it hard for anybody to know where to go for what. Finally, some members were commenting on tasks using 10-word instant messages, without explaining whether their message was an opinion or a request for action.

Eventually, the team and I created norms around the best, most proper use of every communication channel. To see what we built, refer to the exhibit "Setting collaboration channel norms."

Using this chart as your template, set guidelines for your own team. As I discuss in my book *Digital Body Language*, I recommend scheduling a meeting with the sole purpose of having a norm-establishing discussion. To foster an open dialogue, frame the meeting as a group brainstorm and working session. Here are a few questions to get the conversation going:

1. What's been the most collaborative experience you've had in each of these channels?

    – Instant messaging (Microsoft Teams, Slack, Skype, etc.)

Idea in Brief

The Problem

As work shifts from remote to hybrid, many of the norms around digital communication that we've established with our teams need to change too. One study reported that more than 70% of office workers have experienced unclear communication from their colleagues. Without clear rules for how to engage, employees waste time and money deciphering poorly composed or confusing messages.

The Solution

Having a detailed digital communication guide will help ensure that everyone on your team is on the same page and has the same expectations—regardless of who is working from where. In effective norm-setting conversations, teams decide together when to use each communication channel and come up with ways to make the new rules stick.

- – Email

- – Video calls

- – Texting (if applicable)

2. Based on these positive experiences, what are the norms that we want to set up for each channel? (See the rightmost column for specific examples.) As you set up these guidelines, think about message length, complexity, and response time.

   - – How long is too long for an instant message?

   - – Do we want to limit the number of people in a group chat?

   - – When (if ever) is it appropriate to text someone?

   - – What is the expected response time for emails?

Setting collaboration channel norms

Tool	When to use	Response time	Norms
Instant messenger (IM)	Time-sensitive, urgent messages Short and simple conversations	ASAP	Use with fewer than six people (otherwise call) Set your availability Avoid complicated questions or conversations that require visuals
Email	Provide directional, important, and timely information Ensure there's a record of your communication Direct the receiver to an online source for more information	<24 hours; priority dependent	Use identifiers in the subject line for urgency and response expectation Use to share attachments Avoid when immediate response is required Not for random chitchat
Video call	Use for meetings, including external ones that could benefit from visual interaction (e.g., project check-ins, introductions, deck sharing)	Schedule in advance; priority dependent	Use mute if you're not talking Meeting host clarifies if video functionality is required for participation Record calls for those who miss them
Text	Time-sensitive, urgent messages Only use if you were unable to reach the person via other channels	Within 30 minutes if between 7 a.m. and 7 p.m.; priority dependent	Use can be adjusted if it is the preferred communication for your manager Avoid texting during meetings/working sessions

Source: Erica Dhawan, *Digital Body Language: How to Build Trust and Connection No Matter the Distance* (New York: St Martin's Press, 2021).

3. When we transition to a hybrid office, how will we keep including our remote employees and avoid biases?

4. Since many of us are working asynchronously, how can we communicate when we are working and still respect everyone's personal time?

Once you've established your team's communication norms, the hard part is making sure they stick—people tend to revert to old habits. Mindful of this tendency, I worked with the team to identify two or three channel advocates whose role was to encourage best practices within each channel and give shout-outs to those modeling the right behaviors.

We also developed a practice designed to eliminate situations in which individuals send duplicate content across multiple channels. To do this, we rolled out the hashtag #killduplication. If someone doesn't follow the latest hybrid collaboration norms, team members are encouraged to respond with "#killduplication" to make it less of a callout and more of a lighthearted way to reinforce the desired behavior. The #killduplication hashtag is now a staple of the team culture, helping eliminate wasted time and encouraging colleagues to optimize the use of each digital medium.

We are in the midst of a major transition from remote to hybrid work. As this shift is happening, it's essential for managers to establish norms for digital communication with their teams. Having a detailed guide will help ensure that everyone is on the same page and has the same expectations—regardless of who is working from where.

Adapted from hbr.org, May 7, 2021. Reprint H06C87

5

Visualizations That Really Work

by Scott Berinato

Not long ago, the ability to create smart data visualizations, or dataviz, was a nice-to-have skill. For the most part, it benefited design- and data-minded managers who made a deliberate decision to invest in acquiring it. That's changed. Now visual communication is a must-have skill for all managers, because more and more often, it's the only way to make sense of the work they do.

Data is the primary force behind this shift. Decision-making increasingly relies on data, which comes at us with such overwhelming velocity and in such volume that we can't comprehend it without some layer of abstraction, such as a visual one. A typical example: At Boeing the managers of the Osprey program need to improve the efficiency of the aircraft's takeoffs and landings. But each time the Osprey gets off the ground or touches back down, its sensors create a terabyte of data. Ten takeoffs and landings produce as much data as is held in the Library of

Congress. Without visualization, detecting the inefficiencies hidden in the patterns and anomalies of that data would be an impossible slog.

But even information that's not statistical demands visual expression. Complex systems—business process workflows, for example, or the way customers move through a store—are hard to understand, much less fix, if you can't first see them.

Thanks to the internet and a growing number of affordable tools, translating information into visuals is now easy (and cheap) for everyone, regardless of data skills or design skills. This is largely a positive development. One drawback, though, is that it reinforces the impulse to "click and viz" without first thinking about your purpose and goals. *Convenient* is a tempting replacement for good, but it will lead to charts that are merely adequate or, worse, ineffective. Automatically converting spreadsheet cells into a chart only visualizes pieces of a spreadsheet; it doesn't capture an idea. As the presentation expert Nancy Duarte puts it, "Don't project the idea that you're showing a chart. Project the idea that you're showing a reflection of human activity, of things people did to make a line go up and down. It's not 'Here are our Q3 financial results,' it's 'Here's where we missed our targets.'"

Managers who want to get better at making charts often start by learning rules. When should I use a bar chart? How many colors are too many? Where should the key go? Do I have to start my *y*-axis at zero? Visual grammar is important and useful—but knowing it doesn't guarantee that you'll make good charts. To start with chart-making rules is to forgo strategy for execution; it's to pack for a trip without knowing where you're going.

Idea in Brief

Context

Knowledge workers need greater visual literacy than they used to, because so much data—and so many ideas—are now presented graphically. But few of us have been taught data-visualization skills.

Tools Are Fine . . .

Inexpensive tools allow anyone to perform simple tasks such as importing spreadsheet data into a bar chart. But that means it's easy to create terrible charts. Visualization can be so much more: It's an agile, powerful way to explore ideas and communicate information.

. . . But Strategy Is Key

Don't jump straight to execution. Instead, first think about what you're representing—ideas or data? Then consider your purpose: Do you want to inform, persuade, or explore? The answers will suggest what tools and resources you need.

Your visual communication will prove far more successful if you begin by acknowledging that it is not a lone action but, rather, several activities, each of which requires distinct types of planning, resources, and skills. The typology I offer here was created as a reaction to my making the very mistake I just described: The book from which this article is adapted started out as something like a rule book. But after exploring the history of visualization, the exciting state of visualization research, and smart ideas from experts and pioneers, I reconsidered the project. We didn't need another rule book; we needed a way to think about the increasingly crucial discipline of visual communication as a whole.

The typology described in this article is simple. By answering just two questions, you can set yourself up to succeed.

The Two Questions

To start thinking visually, consider the nature and purpose of your visualization: Is the information *conceptual* or *data-driven*? Am I *declaring* something or *exploring* something?

If you know the answers to these questions, you can plan what resources and tools you'll need and begin to discern what type of visualization will help you achieve your goals most effectively.

	Conceptual	Data-driven
Focus	*Ideas*	*Statistics*
Goals	*Simplify, teach* "Here's how our organization is structured."	*Inform, enlighten* "Here are our revenues for the past two years."

The first question is the simpler of the two, and the answer is usually obvious. Either you're visualizing qualitative information or you're plotting quantitative information: ideas or statistics. But notice that the question is about the information itself, not the forms you might ultimately use to show it. For example, the classic Gartner Hype Cycle uses a traditionally data-driven form—a line chart—but no actual data. It's a concept.

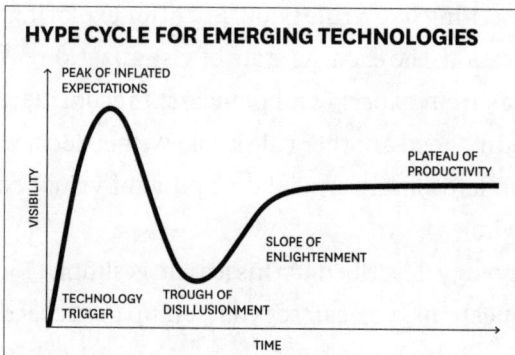

HYPE CYCLE FOR EMERGING TECHNOLOGIES

If the first question identifies what you *have,* the second elicits what you're *doing:* either communicating information (declarative) or trying to figure something out (exploratory).

	Declarative	Exploratory
Focus	*Documenting, designing*	*Prototyping, iterating, interacting, automating*
Goals	*Affirm* "Here is our budget by department."	*Confirm* "Let's see if marketing investments contributed to rising profits." *Discover* "What would we see if we visualized customer purchases by gender, location, and purchase amount in real time?"

Managers most often work with declarative visualizations, which make a statement, usually to an audience in a formal setting. If you have a spreadsheet workbook full of sales data and you're using it to show quarterly sales in a presentation, your purpose is declarative.

But let's say your boss wants to understand why the sales team's performance has lagged lately. You suspect that seasonal cycles have caused the dip, but you're not sure. Now your purpose is exploratory, and you'll use the same data to create visuals that will confirm or refute your hypothesis. The audience is usually yourself or a small team. If your hypothesis is confirmed, you may well show your boss a declarative visualization, saying, "Here's what's happening to sales."

Exploratory visualizations are actually of two kinds. In the example above, you were testing a hypothesis. But suppose you don't have an idea about why performance is lagging—you don't know what you're looking for. You want to mine your workbook to see what patterns, trends, and anomalies emerge. What will you see, for example, when you measure sales performance in relation to the size of the region a salesperson manages? What happens if you compare seasonal trends in various geographies? How does weather affect sales? Such data brainstorming can deliver fresh insights. Big strategic questions—Why are revenues falling? Where can we find efficiencies? How do customers interact with us?—can benefit from a discovery-focused exploratory visualization.

The Four Types

The nature and purpose questions combine in a classic 2 × 2 to define four types of visual communication: idea illustration, idea generation, visual discovery, and everyday dataviz.

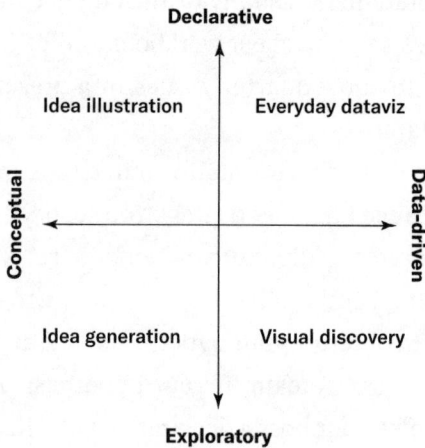

Idea illustration

Info type	Process, framework
Typical setting	Presentations, teaching
Primary skills	Design, editing
Goals	Learning, simplifying, explaining

We might call this quadrant the "consultants' corner." Consultants can't resist process diagrams, cycle diagrams, and the like. At their best, idea illustrations clarify complex ideas by drawing on our ability to understand metaphors (trees, bridges) and simple design conventions (circles, hierarchies). Org charts and decision trees are classic examples of idea illustration. So is the 2×2 that frames this article.

Idea illustration demands clear and simple design, but its reliance on metaphor invites unnecessary adornment. Because the discipline and boundaries of data sets aren't built in to idea illustration, they must be imposed. The focus should be on clear communication, structure, and the logic of the ideas. The most useful skills here are similar to what a text editor brings to a manuscript—the ability to pare things down to their essence. Some design skills will be useful too, whether they're your own or hired.

Suppose a company engages consultants to help its R&D group find inspiration in other industries. The consultants use a technique called the *pyramid search*—a way to get information from experts in other fields close to your own, who point you to the top experts in their fields, who point you to experts in still other fields, who then help you find the experts in those fields, and so on.

It's actually tricky to explain, so the consultants may use visualization to help. How does a pyramid search work? It looks something like this:

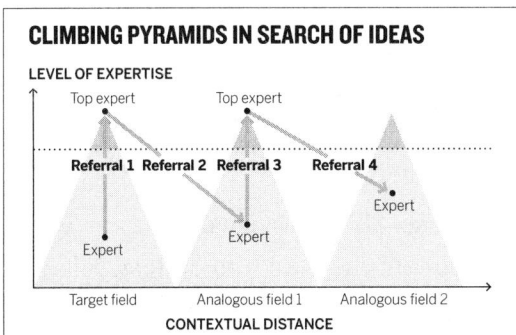

CLIMBING PYRAMIDS IN SEARCH OF IDEAS

LEVEL OF EXPERTISE

Top expert   Top expert

Referral 1   Referral 2   Referral 3   Referral 4

Expert

Expert

Expert

Target field   Analogous field 1   Analogous field 2

CONTEXTUAL DISTANCE

The axes use conventions that we can grasp immediately: industries plotted near to far and expertise mapped low to high. The pyramid shape itself shows the relative rarity of top experts compared with lower-level ones. Words in the title—"climbing" and "pyramids"—help us grasp the idea quickly. Finally, the designer didn't succumb to a temptation to decorate: The pyramids aren't literal, three-dimensional, sandstone-colored objects.

Too often, idea illustration doesn't go that well, and you end up with something like this:

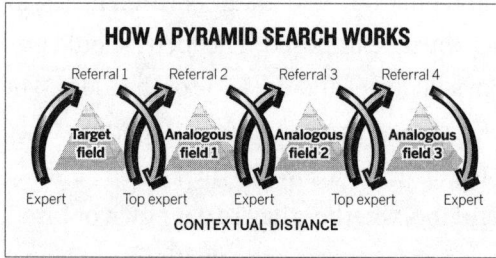

HOW A PYRAMID SEARCH WORKS

Referral 1   Referral 2   Referral 3   Referral 4

Target field   Analogous field 1   Analogous field 2   Analogous field 3

Expert   Top expert   Expert   Top expert   Expert

CONTEXTUAL DISTANCE

Here the color gradient, the drop shadows, and the 3-D pyramids distract us from the idea. The arrows don't actually demonstrate how a pyramid search works. And experts and top experts are placed on the same plane instead of at different heights to convey relative status.

Idea generation

Info type	Complex, undefined
Typical setting	Working session, brainstorming
Primary skills	Team-building, facilitation
Goals	Problem-solving, discovery, innovation

Managers may not think of visualization as a tool to support idea generation, but they use it to brainstorm all the time—on whiteboards, on butcher paper, or, classically, on the back of a napkin. Like idea illustration, idea generation relies on conceptual metaphors, but it takes place in more-informal settings, such as off-sites, strategy sessions, and early-phase innovation projects. It's used to find new ways of seeing how the business works and to answer complex managerial challenges: restructuring an organization, coming up with a new business process, codifying a system for making decisions.

Although idea generation can be done alone, it benefits from collaboration and borrows from design thinking—gathering as many diverse points of view and visual approaches as possible before homing in on one and refining it. Jon Kolko, the founder and director of the Austin Center for Design and the author of *Well-Designed: How to Use Empathy to Create Products People Love,* fills the whiteboard walls of his office with conceptual, exploratory visualizations. "It's our go-to method for thinking through complexity," he says. "Sketching is this effort to work through ambiguity and muddiness and come to crispness." Managers who are good at leading teams, facilitating brainstorming sessions, and encouraging and then capturing creative thinking will do well in this quadrant. Design skills and editing are less important here, and sometimes counterproductive. When you're seeking breakthroughs, editing is the opposite of what you need, and you should think in rapid sketches; refined designs will just slow you down.

Suppose a marketing team is holding an off-site. The team members need to come up with a way to show executives their proposed strategy for going upmarket. An hour-long whiteboard session yields several approaches and ideas (none of which are erased) for presenting the strategy. Ultimately, one approach gains purchase with the team, which thinks it best captures the key point: Get fewer customers to spend much more. The white-board looks something like this:

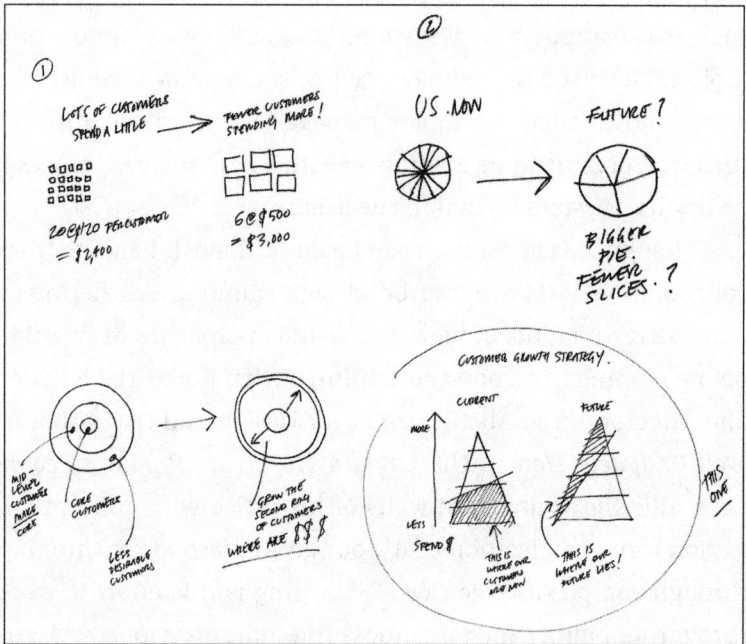

Of course, visuals that emerge from idea generation often lead to more formally designed and presented idea illustrations.

Visual discovery

Info type	Big data, complex, dynamic
Typical setting	Working sessions, testing, analysis
Primary skills	Business intelligence, programming, paired analysis
Goals	Trend spotting, sense making, deep analysis

This is the most complicated quadrant, because in truth it holds two categories. Recall that we originally separated exploratory purposes into two kinds: testing a hypothesis and mining for patterns, trends, and anomalies. The former is focused, whereas the latter is more flexible. The bigger and more complex the data, and the less you know going in, the more open-ended the work.

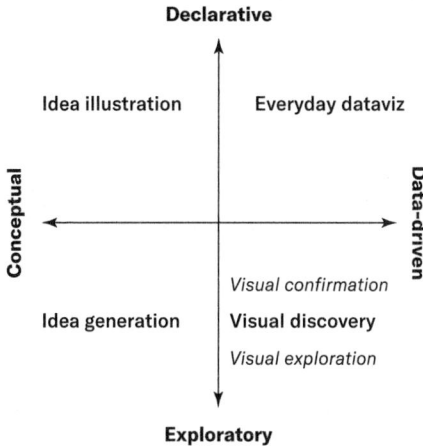

Visual confirmation. You're answering one of two questions with this kind of project: Is what I suspect actually true? or What are some other ways of depicting this idea?

The scope of the data tends to be manageable, and the chart types you're likely to use are common—although when trying to depict things in new ways, you may venture into some less-common types. Confirmation usually doesn't happen in a formal setting; it's the work you do to find the charts you want to create for presentations. That means your time will shift away from design and toward prototyping that allows you to rapidly iterate on the dataviz. Some skill at manipulating spreadsheets and knowledge of programs or sites that enable swift prototyping are useful here.

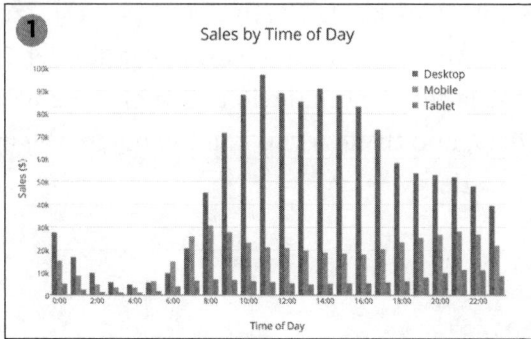

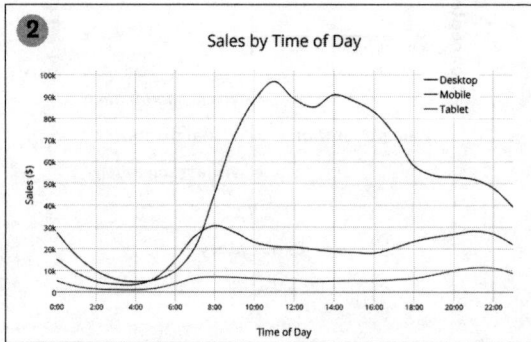

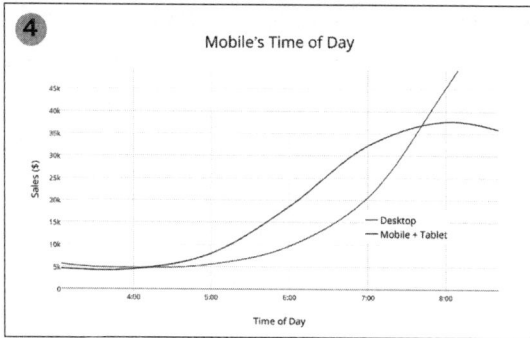

Suppose a marketing manager believes that at certain times of the day more customers shop his site on mobile devices than on desktops, but his marketing programs aren't designed to take advantage of that. He loads some data into an online tool (called Datawrapper) to see if he's right (1 on previous page).

He can't yet confirm or refute his hypothesis. He can't tell much of anything, but he's prototyping and using a tool that makes it easy to try different views into the data. He works fast; design is not a concern. He tries a line chart instead of a bar chart (2).

Now he's seeing something, but working with three variables still doesn't quite get at the mobile-versus-desktop view he wants, so he tries again with two variables (3). Each time he iterates, he evaluates whether he can confirm his original hypothesis: At certain times of day more customers are shopping on mobile devices than on desktops.

On the fourth try he zooms in and confirms his hypothesis (4).

New software tools mean this type of visualization is easier than ever before: They're making data analysts of us all.

Visual exploration. Open-ended data-driven visualizations tend to be the province of data scientists and business intelligence analysts, although new tools have begun to engage general managers in visual exploration. It's exciting to try, because it often produces insights that can't be gleaned any other way.

Because we don't know what we're looking for, these visuals tend to plot data more inclusively. In extreme cases, this kind of project may combine multiple data sets or load dynamic, real-time data into a system that updates automatically. Statistical modeling benefits from visual exploration.

Exploration also lends itself to interactivity: Managers can adjust parameters, inject new data sources, and continually revisualize. Complex data sometimes also suits specialized and unusual visualization, such as *force-directed diagrams* that show how networks cluster, or topographical plots.

Function trumps form here: Analytical, programming, data management, and business intelligence skills are more crucial than the ability to create presentable charts. Not surprisingly, this half of the quadrant is where managers are most likely to call in experts to help set up systems to wrangle data and create visualizations that fit their analytic goals.

Anmol Garg, a data scientist at Tesla Motors, has used visual exploration to tap into the vast amount of sensor data the company's cars produce. Garg created an interactive chart that shows the pressure in a car's tires over time. In true exploratory form, he and his team first created the visualizations and then found a variety of uses for them: to see whether tires are properly inflated when a car leaves the factory, how often customers reinflate them, and how long customers take to respond to a low-pressure alert; to find leak rates; and to do some predictive modeling on when tires are likely to go flat. The pressure of all four tires is visualized on a scatter plot, which, however inscrutable to a general audience, is clear to its intended audience.

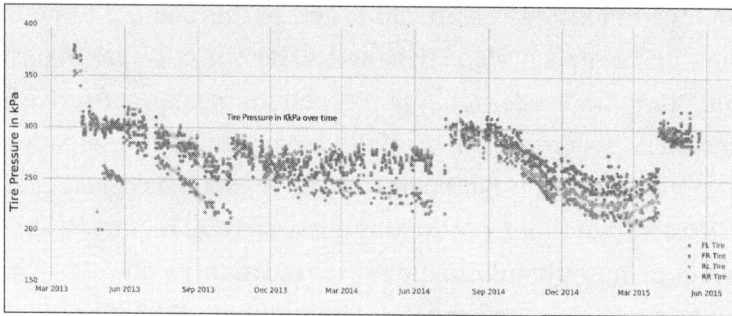

Garg was exploring data to find insights that could be gleaned only through visuals. "We're dealing with terabytes of data all the time," he says. "You can't find anything looking at spreadsheets and querying databases. It has to be visual." For presentations to the executive team, Garg translates these exploration sessions into the kinds of simpler charts discussed below. "Management loves seeing visualizations," he says.

Everyday dataviz

Info type	Simple, low volume
Typical setting	Formal, presentations
Primary skills	Design, storytelling
Goals	Affirming, setting context

Whereas data scientists do most of the work on visual exploration, managers do most of the work on everyday visualizations. This quadrant comprises the basic charts and graphs you normally paste from a spreadsheet into a presentation. They are usually simple—line charts, bar charts, pies, and scatterplots.

"Simple" is the key. Ideally, the visualization will communicate a single message, charting only a few variables. And the goal is straightforward: affirming and setting context. Simplicity is primarily a design challenge, so design skills are important. Clarity and consistency make these charts most effective in the setting where they're typically used: a formal presentation. In a presentation, time is constrained. A poorly designed chart will waste that time by provoking questions that require the presenter to interpret information that's meant to be obvious. If an everyday dataviz can't speak for itself, it has failed—just like a joke whose punch line has to be explained.

That's not to say that declarative charts shouldn't generate discussion. But the discussion should be about the idea in the chart, not the chart itself.

Suppose an HR VP will be presenting to the rest of the executive committee about the company's health care costs. She wants to convey that the growth of these costs has slowed significantly, creating an opportunity to invest in additional health care services.

The VP has read an online report about this trend that includes a link to some government data. She downloads the data and clicks on the line chart option in Excel. She has her viz in a few seconds. But because this is for a presentation, she asks a designer colleague to add detail from the data set to give a more comprehensive view.

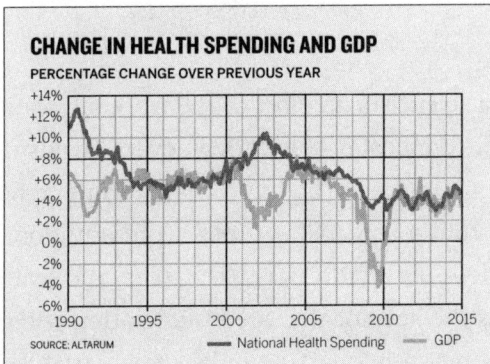

CHANGE IN HEALTH SPENDING AND GDP
PERCENTAGE CHANGE OVER PREVIOUS YEAR

SOURCE: ALTARUM — National Health Spending — GDP

This is a well-designed, accurate chart, but it's probably not the right one. The executive committee doesn't need two decades' worth of historical context to discuss the company's strategy for employee benefits investments. The point the VP wants to make is that cost increases have slowed over the past few years. Is that clearly communicated here?

In general, when it takes more than a few seconds to digest the data in a chart, the chart will work better on paper or on a personal-device screen, for someone who's not expected to listen to a presentation while trying to take in so much information. For example, health care policy makers might benefit from seeing this chart in advance of a hearing at which they'll discuss these long-term trends.

Our VP needs something cleaner for her context. She could make her point as simply as this:

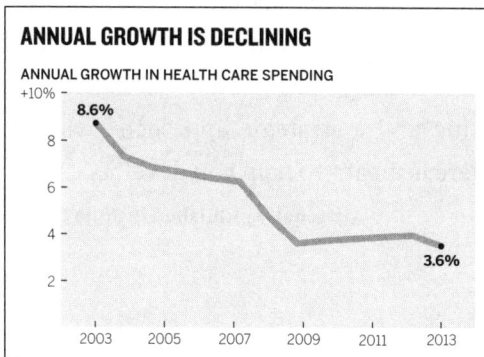

ANNUAL GROWTH IS DECLINING

ANNUAL GROWTH IN HEALTH CARE SPENDING

Simplicity like this takes some discipline—and courage—to achieve. The impulse is to include everything you know. Busy charts communicate the idea that you've been just that—busy. "Look at all the data I have and the work I've done," they seem to say. But that's not the VP's goal. She wants to persuade her colleagues to invest in new programs. With this chart, she won't have to utter a word for the executive team to understand the trend. She has clearly established a foundation for her recommendations.

. . .

In some ways, "data visualization" is a terrible term. It seems to reduce the construction of good charts to a mechanical procedure. It evokes the tools and methodology required to create rather than the creation itself. It's like calling *Moby-Dick* a "word sequentialization" or *The Starry Night* a "pigment distribution."

It also reflects an ongoing obsession in the dataviz world with process over outcomes. Visualization is merely a process. What we actually do when we make a good chart is get at some truth and move people to feel it—to see what couldn't be seen before. To change minds. To cause action.

Some basic common grammar will improve our ability to communicate visually. But good outcomes require a broader understanding and a strategic approach—which the typology described here is meant to help you develop.

Originally published in June 2016. Reprint R1606H

6

How to Become an Authentic Speaker

by Nick Morgan

A t a companywide sales meeting, Carol, a vice president of sales, strides energetically to the podium, pauses for a few seconds to look at the audience, and then tells a story from her days as a field rep. She deftly segues from her anecdote to a positive assessment of the company's sales outlook for the year, supplementing her speech with colorful slides showing strong growth and exciting new products in the pipeline. While describing those products, she accents her words with animated gestures.

Having rehearsed carefully in front of a small audience of trusted colleagues, all of whom liked her message and her energy, she now confidently delivers the closer: Walking to the edge of the stage, she scans the room and challenges her listeners to commit to a stretch sales goal that will put many of them in the annual winners' circle.

But Carol senses that something's amiss. The audience isn't exhibiting the kind of enthusiasm needed to get the year off to a great start. She begins to panic: What's happening? Is there anything she can do to salvage the situation?

We all know a Carol. (You may be one yourself.) We've all heard speeches like hers, presentations in which the speaker is apparently doing all the right things, yet something—something we can't quite identify—is wrong.

If asked about these speeches, we might describe them as "calculated," "insincere," "not real," or "phoned in." We probably wouldn't be able to say exactly why the performance wasn't compelling. The speaker just didn't seem *authentic*.

In today's difficult economy, and especially in the aftermath of numerous scandals involving individual executives, employees and shareholders are more skeptical than ever. Authenticity—including the ability to communicate authentically with others—has become an important leadership attribute. When leaders have it, they can inspire their followers to make extraordinary efforts on behalf of their organizations. When they don't, cynicism prevails and few employees do more than the minimum necessary to get by.

In my 22 years of working as a communications coach, I have seen again and again how hard it is for managers to come across in public communications as authentic—even when they passionately believe their message. Why is this kind of communication so difficult? Why can't people just stand up and tell the truth?

What Science Teaches Us

The answer lies in recent research into the ways our brains perceive and process communication. We all know by now the power of nonverbal communication—what I call the "second

Idea in Brief

You rehearsed your speech thoroughly—and mastered that all-important body language. But when you delivered the talk, you sensed little enthusiasm in your audience.

What's going on? You're probably coming across as artificial. The reason: When we rehearse specific body language elements, we use them incorrectly during the actual speech—slightly *after* speaking the associated words. Listeners feel something's wrong, because during natural conversation, body language emerges *before* the associated words.

To demonstrate your authenticity, don't rehearse your body language. Instead, imagine meeting four aims:

- Being open to your audience
- Connecting with your audience
- Being passionate about your topic
- Listening to your audience

When you rehearse this way, you'll genuinely experience these feelings when delivering your speech. Your body language will emerge at the right moment. And your listeners will know you're the real thing.

conversation." If your spoken message and your body language are mismatched, audiences will respond to the nonverbal message every time. Gestures speak louder than words. And that means you *can't* just stand up and tell the truth. You'll often hear someone say in advance of a speech, "I don't want to look over-rehearsed, so I'm going to wing it." But during the presentation his body language will undermine his credibility. Because he's in a stressful situation with no preparation, he'll appear off-kilter. Whatever the message of his words, he'll seem to be learning as he goes—not likely to engender confidence in a leader.

So preparation is important. But the traditional approach—careful rehearsal like Carol's—often doesn't work either. That's because it usually involves specific coaching on nonverbal elements—"maintain eye contact," "spread your arms," "walk out from behind the podium"—that can ultimately make the speaker seem artificial. The audience can see the wheels turning in her head as she goes through the motions.

Why does this calculated body language come off as inauthentic? Here's where the brain research comes in. We're learning that in human beings the second, nonverbal conversation actually starts *first,* in the instant after an emotion or an impulse fires deep within the brain but before it has been articulated. Indeed, research shows that people's natural and unstudied gestures are often indicators of what they will think and say next.

You might say that words are after-the-fact explanations of why we just gestured as we did. Think of something as simple as a hug: The impulse to embrace someone begins *before* the thought that you're glad to see him or her has fully formed, much less been expressed aloud. Or think about a typical conversation: Reinforcement, contradiction, and commentary arise first in gesture. We nod vigorously, shake our heads, roll our eyes, all of which express our reactions more immediately—and more powerfully—than words can.

If gesture precedes conscious thought and thought precedes words—even if by no more than a tiny fraction of a second—that changes our thinking about speech preparation. When coached in the traditional way, rehearsing specific gestures one by one, speakers end up employing those gestures at the same time that—or even slightly after—they speak the associated words. Although audiences are not consciously aware of this unnatural sequence, their innate ability to read body language leads them to feel that something's wrong—that the speaker is inauthentic.

"Rehearsing" Authenticity

So if neither casual spontaneity nor traditional rehearsal leads to compelling communication, how can you prepare for an important presentation? You have to tap into the basic impulses underlying your speech. These should include four powerful aims: to be open, to connect, to be passionate, and to listen. Each of these aims informs nearly all successful presentations.

Rehearse your speech with them in mind. Try practicing it four ways, adopting the mindset of each aim in turn, feeling it more than thinking about it. Forget about rehearsing specific gestures. If you are able to sincerely realize these feelings, your body language will take care of itself, emerging naturally and at the right moment. (The approach described here may also lead you to refine some of your verbal message, to make it accord with your nonverbal one.) When you actually deliver the speech, continue to focus on the four underlying aims.

Note the paradox here. This method is designed to achieve authenticity through the mastery of a calculated process. But authenticity arises from the four aims, or what I call "intents," that I have mentioned. If you can physically and emotionally embody all four, you'll achieve the perceived *and* real authenticity that creates a powerful bond with listeners.

What Underlies an Authentic Speech

Creating that bond isn't easy. Let me offer some advice for tapping into each of the four intents.

A Speech Is Not an Essay

by John Coleman

For those new to public speaking, the tendency to mimic the forms and features of writing can be crippling.

The average adult reads 300 words per minute, but people can only follow speech closely at around 150 to 160 words per minute. Similarly, studies have shown that auditory memory is inferior to visual memory, and while most of us can read for hours, our ability to focus on a speech is more constrained. It's important, then, to write brief and clear speeches. Ten minutes of speaking is only about 1,300 words, and while written texts—which can be reviewed, studied, and reexamined—can be subtle and nuanced, the spoken word is followed in the moment and must be appropriately short, sweet, and to the point.

It's also important to signpost and review key points within your speech. In a written essay, readers can revisit confusing passages or missed points. But once you lose someone in a speech, that person may be lost for good. In your introduction, state your thesis and then lay out the structure of your speech (e.g., "We'll see this in three ways: x, y, and z"). Then open each new point with a signpost to orient your listeners, with words such as "to begin,"

The intent to be open with your audience

This is the first and in some ways the most important thing to focus on in rehearsing a speech, because if you come across as closed, your listeners will perceive you as defensive—as if they somehow represent a threat. Not much chance for communication there.

How can you become more open? Try to imagine giving your presentation to someone with whom you're completely relaxed—your spouse, a close friend, your child. Notice what that mental picture looks like but particularly what it *feels* "secondly," and "finally," and close each point with a similar sign-post (e.g., "So we now see, the first element of success is x"). This lack of subtlety would be repetitive and inelegant in a written document, but it is essential to a speech.

Similarly, the subtleties of complex argumentation and statistical analysis can be compelling in an essay, but in a speech you should keep the statistics to a minimum and opt for longer and more vivid stories. Lead or end an important point with the relevant statistics. But never fall into reciting strings of numbers or citations.

And remember that when you're speaking, your audience doesn't have the benefit of commas, quotation marks, paragraph breaks, or exclamation points. Instead, use your voice, your hand gestures, your pace, and even your posture and position on stage to give your speech texture and range. Vary your level of excitement, your tone, and your volume for emphasis. Use hand gestures consciously and in keeping with the points you're trying to make. Between main points, walk to another spot on the stage to indicate that a new part of your presentation is beginning.

If you're a great writer, don't assume that talent will translate to the spoken word. "A speech is not an essay on its hind legs," as communications professor Bob Frank says, and great speechwriters and public speakers adapt accordingly.

---

like. This is the state you need to be in if you are to have an authentic rapport with your audience.

If it's hard to create this mental image, try the real thing. Find a patient friend and push yourself to be open with him or her. Notice what that scene looks like and, again, how you feel. Don't over-intellectualize: This is a bit like practicing a golf swing or a tennis serve. Although you might make tiny mental notes about what you're doing, they shouldn't get in the way of recognizing a feeling that you can try to replicate later.

Openness immediately feels risky to many people. I worked with a CEO who was passionate about his work, but his audiences didn't respond. He realized that he'd learned as a boy not to show emotion precisely about the things that meant the most to him. We had to replace this felt experience with one of talking to a close friend he was excited to see.

Let's go back to Carol (a composite of several clients). As she works on feeling more open in her presentations, her face begins to light up with a big smile when she speaks, and her shoulders relax. She realizes that without meaning to, she has come across as so serious that she has alienated her audiences.

A change in nonverbal behavior can affect the spoken message. Over and over, I've seen clients begin speaking more comfortably—and more authentically—as the intent to be more open physically led to a more candid expression of their thoughts.

The intent to connect with your audience

Once you begin to feel open, and you've stored away the memory of what it looks and feels like, you're ready to practice the speech again, this time focusing on the audience. Think about wanting— *needing*—to engage your listeners. Imagine that a young child you know well isn't heeding you. You want to capture that child's attention however you can. You don't strategize—you simply do what feels natural and appropriate. You increase the intensity or volume of your voice or move closer.

You also want to *keep* your audience's attention. Don't let listeners slide away into their thoughts instead of following yours. Here, you might transform your young child into a teenager and imagine yearning to keep this easily distractible listener focused on your words.

If openness is the ante that lets you into the game, connection is what keeps the audience playing. Now that Carol is intent on being connected with her listeners, she realizes that she typically waits too long—in fact, until the very end of her speech—to make contact with them. She begins her next presentation by reaching out to audience members who have contributed significantly to the company's sales success, establishing a connection that continues throughout her speech.

The intent to be passionate about your topic

Ask yourself what it is that you feel deeply about. What's at stake? What results do you want your presentation to produce? Are you excited about the prospects of your company? Worried that they look bleak? Determined to improve them?

Focus not on what you want to say but on why you're giving the speech and how you feel about that. Let the underlying emotion come out (once you've identified it, you won't need to force it) in every word you deliver during this round of rehearsal. Then raise the stakes for yourself: Imagine that somebody in the audience has the power to take everything away from you unless you win him or her over with your passionate argument.

I worked with a senior partner at a consulting firm who was planning to talk to her colleagues about the things at the firm she valued and wanted to pass on to the next generation as she got ready to retire. Her speech, when she began practicing it, was a crystal clear but dull commentary on the importance of commitment and hard work. As she began focusing on the emotion beneath the speech, she recalled how her mother, a dancer, had instilled in her the value of persisting no matter what the obstacles. She decided to acknowledge her mother in her talk. She said that her mother, then 92, had never let the pain and difficulties she had experienced during her career obscure her joy in performing. Although the speaker shed most of her tears during rehearsal, her passion transformed the talk into something memorable.

Somewhat more prosaically, Carol begins to think about what she's passionate about—her determination to beat a close competitor—and how that might inform her presentations. She realizes that this passion fuels her energy and excitement about her job. She infuses her next speech with some of that passion and immediately comes across as more human and engaging.

The intent to "listen" to your audience

Now begin thinking about what your listeners are likely to be feeling when you step up to begin your presentation. Are they excited about the future? Worried about bad sales news? Hopeful they can keep their jobs after the merger? As you practice, imagine yourself watching them very closely, looking for signs of their response to you.

Of course, your intent to discover the audience's emotional state will be most important during the actual presentation. Usually your listeners won't actually be talking to you, but they will be sending you nonverbal messages that you'll need to pick up and respond to.

This isn't as hard as it may sound. As a fellow member of the human race, you are as expert as your audience in reading body language—if you have an intent to do so. As you read the messages your listeners are sending with their bodies, you may want

to pick up the pace, vary your language, even change or eliminate parts of your talk. If this leads you to involve the audience
in a real dialogue—say, by asking an impromptu question—so
much the better.

If time has been set aside for questions at the end of your presentation, you'll want to listen to the audience with your whole
body, keeping yourself physically and psychologically still in
the way you might when someone is telling you something so
important that you dare not miss a word. Without thinking
about it, you'll find yourself leaning forward or nodding your
head—gestures that would appear unnatural if you were doing
them because you'd been told to.

Of course, listening to and responding to an audience in the
middle of your speech requires that you have your material down
cold. But you can also take what your listeners tell you and use it
to improve future presentations. I worked with a sales executive
who had been so successful that she began touring the world in
order to share her secrets with others. In listening to audiences,
paying attention to their bodies as well as their words, she began
to realize that they didn't just want to receive what she had to
say; they wanted to give her something in return. The executive's speeches were inspiring, and her listeners wanted to thank
her. So we designed a brief but meaningful ceremony near the
end of her speech that allowed the audience members to get up,
interact with one another, and give back to the speaker some of
the inspiration she was giving them.

Consider Carol once again. Because of her intent to pick up
on her listeners' emotions, Carol begins to realize over the
course of several speeches that she has been wrongly assuming that her salespeople share her sense of urgency about their

major competitor. She resolves to spend more time at the beginning of her next presentation explaining why stretch goals are important. This response to her listeners' state of mind, when combined with her own desire to be open, connected, and passionate, strengthens her growing ability to come across as—and be—an authentic speaker.

Originally published in November 2008. Reprint R0811H

7

What People Get Wrong About Psychological Safety

by Amy C. Edmondson and Michaela J. Kerrissey

P sychological safety, which means having an environment where people feel safe to speak up, was once an obscure term in psychology and management research. Today the concept is downright popular. Countless managers, consultants, and training companies have worked hard to create psychologically safe workplaces, and thousands of articles have been devoted to the topic.

As researchers with considerable expertise in this area, we celebrate organizations' recognition that their ability to increase quality, spur innovation, and boost performance depends on their employees' input. Indeed, the research evidence that psychological safety improves performance is extensive and robust.

However, as the popularity of psychological safety has grown, so too have misconceptions about it. As a result, many executives and consultants, even those who are ardent supporters of psychological safety, have become frustrated by distorted or incorrect ideas and expectations surrounding it that get in the way of progress. For instance, leaders have told us about constructive debates that were stymied when participants whose ideas received pushback labeled the process psychologically unsafe. This kind of misinterpretation of the term can harm organizations. And if it persists, it can undermine the very purpose of psychological safety: to enhance learning and performance.

Leaders who truly understand what psychological safety is—and isn't—communicate the concept to their teams clearly, stop incorrect assumptions before they gain destructive force, and keep people focused on the value to be gained from candor. We've written this article to aid leaders in that effort. We describe six misconceptions, explaining why each gets in the way and how to counter it, and then offer a blueprint for building the kind of strong, learning-oriented work environment that is crucial for success in an uncertain world.

Misconception 1: Psychological Safety Means Being Nice

Nicole, a consultant in the Netherlands, recently told us that she kept hearing clients say things like "We have a psychologically safe team; we know this because we never argue." As an expert in psychological safety, she recognized this as a red flag. Indeed, thinking that psychological safety is about being nice or feeling comfortable is one of the most common misconceptions. We see it in companies and schools alike. For instance,

Idea in Brief

The Problem

Psychological safety is widely recognized as essential for high-performing teams, but it's often misunderstood. Many leaders mistakenly equate it with comfort, consensus, or the absence of accountability—leading to cultures that avoid conflict or underperform.

The Insight

True psychological safety isn't about being nice or avoiding hard conversations. It's about creating an environment where people feel safe to take interpersonal risks—such as speaking up, admitting mistakes, or challenging the status quo—because they trust they won't be punished or humiliated for doing so. The goal is not comfort, but candor and continuous learning.

The Payoff

When psychological safety is properly understood and implemented, teams become more innovative and resilient, engage in richer dialogue, and are able to adapt more quickly to fast-changing business environments.

a graduate student we know asked to shift from in-person to virtual attendance because she found participating in a large class uncomfortable. The accommodation, she said, was important for her psychological safety.

Here's the problem: Nice in this context is code for "Don't say what you really think (unless it happens to be nice)." It's essentially the opposite of candor. Of course, if you think your colleague's presentation was brilliant and compelling, say so! It will unquestionably be appreciated and foster a positive climate. But if the presentation fell short, it's important that you say so as clearly and constructively as possible. For organizations to succeed today, their people must be continually learning, and that process is often uncomfortable.

Safety and comfort are not synonymous. Safety is the condition of being protected from danger, harm, or injury. Comfort is a state of ease and freedom from pain. Wanting to be nice, people avoid being honest and, whether they realize it or not, collude in producing ignorance and mediocrity. Because without candid feedback and open sharing of information—bad and good—coordination, quality, and learning on a team or a project suffer. Teams that don't surface hard truths perform worse than those that do. Consider the Kennedy administration's disastrous Bay of Pigs decision, which approved an invasion of Cuba by a brigade of Cuban exiles in 1961. Although some experts working for President Kennedy had grave concerns about the plan, they didn't speak up for fear of appearing unsupportive. The resulting catastrophe led Kennedy to insist on a structured process to ensure candor and rigorous debate the next time he faced a serious foreign policy decision. That process contributed to his administration's impressive performance during the Cuban Missile Crisis, in 1962. (See "What You Don't Know About Making Decisions," HBR, September 2001.) Studies of less dramatic work environments show a similar contrast: When people withhold their ideas, questions, and doubts, their team's risk of making mistakes and experiencing failure increases.

We find it helpful to think of psychological safety as a shared sense of *permission for candor*. It's a belief that it's OK to take the interpersonal risks that come with asking questions, admitting mistakes, and disagreeing with a colleague. When psychological safety exists, people believe that sharing hard truths is expected. It allows good debates to happen when they're needed. But it doesn't mean that participants find debates comfortable.

To be clear, we are not advocating for insensitivity. Psychological safety is entirely consistent with kindness, but let's distinguish between being nice and being kind. Nice is the easy way out of a difficult conversation. Kind is being respectful, caring, and honest.

Misconception 2: Psychological Safety Means Getting Your Way

Less common but equally problematic is the misconception people have that psychological safety means their views should prevail. A healthcare executive told us that a staff member had complained, "You didn't support my idea in that meeting, and that made me feel psychologically unsafe."

That employee, along with many other people, did not understand that psychological safety is about making sure leaders or teams hear what people think. It's not about forcing them to agree with what they hear. The goal is to reach a good decision or prevent a defect in a product. It's helpful to think of psychological safety not as a gift for one participant but rather as an environment for the whole team.

Leaders don't need to agree with everyone's input. And they shouldn't tolerate problematic behavior. Sanctions for bullying, harassment, disrespect, and unethical conduct are vital to ensuring a positive learning environment.

Misconception 3: Psychological Safety Means Job Security

Shocked by Google's announcement in January 2023 that it was laying off 12,000 employees, multiple workers posted on social media sites that the action was counter to their company's commitment to psychological safety. In a town hall meeting, one Google employee expressed this sentiment out loud.

But psychological safety doesn't mean freedom *from* lay-offs. It's freedom *to* be constructively candid. Ironically, the employee demonstrated that psychological safety did exist at Google when he stood up and criticized the company to its senior leaders. He believed he could speak up without risking his career or generating negative reactions from colleagues. He didn't save his views for whispered hallway conversations. (Full disclosure: Both authors have performed paid work for companies named in this article—Amy for Google and Microsoft; Michaela for Google.)

Misconception 4: Psychological Safety Requires a Trade-Off with Performance

Some leaders worry that fostering psychological safety among employees will make it hard to address weaknesses and assign accountability for achieving excellence. They seem to think of the two as being on a spectrum, with psychological safety on one end and accountability for performance on the other. But that's wrong.

Psychological safety and accountability are distinct dimensions. To decide which is more important is to impose a false dichotomy. When both are low, performance and morale clearly suffer. And yes, it is possible to have high levels of psychological safety and low performance standards, though that is certainly not a recipe for excellence. In any uncertain environment, superb performance requires a commitment to both high standards *and* psychological safety. That is because psychological safety enables learning—it helps surface information and knowledge vital for competing in a changing world. (See "The Competitive Imperative of Learning," HBR, July–August 2008.) Nonetheless, extensive research shows that not learning in groups is common. People hide information to save face or to be agreeable or both. And teams fall easily into groupthink— where members don't want to disrupt what they erroneously assume is a consensus.

Misconception 5: Psychological Safety Is a Policy

In April 2024 the Rhode Island state senate passed Bill 2473A, the Workplace Psychological Safety Act, which sought to create psychologically safe work environments. It enabled employees to sue their employer for damages if it didn't. (As of this writing, the bill hasn't progressed beyond the state senate.) This piece of legislature reflects the common but misguided belief that organizations should mandate psychological safety. We can't mandate psychological safety any more than we can mandate things like trust and motivation.

Psychological safety is not a quick fix. You can't pull a lever and make it happen. Telling people in a company or on a team that they must have psychological safety "or else" will not produce it. In fact, it's more likely to result in leaders being kept in the dark about what's really going on.

Psychological safety, rather than being created by a policy, is built in a group, interaction by interaction. It takes intention and effort to create a climate of candor. It's particularly helpful when leaders consciously use three tools:

- *Messaging:* Leaders should make statements that highlight the challenges of the situation the organization faces.

- *Modeling:* They must also be role models for asking good questions, listening intently, and acknowledging that it's OK not to know all the answers.

- *Mentoring:* Leaders need to give people feedback on their impact—on how well they invite and respond to others' input—and work to minimize the negative consequences anyone on the team suffers from speaking up.

Developing new skills is harder than adopting a new policy. But it can be done. Many companies invest in materials and programs to help their employees acquire skills for fostering psychological safety. Relatedly, many employee surveys include a psychological safety measure by asking people how much they agree or disagree with statements such as, "If you make a mistake in this team, it's not held against you" and "It is safe to take a risk on this team." Ideally, the data collected is used as fodder for conversations about how to keep improving the work environment.

Misconception 6: Psychological Safety Requires a Top-Down Approach

We often hear people say that an organization's leaders must be the ones to establish psychological safety. It's true that what leaders do matters—they have an enormous impact on a team or an organization's culture. Hierarchy is deeply ingrained in our psyche. People instinctively care what leaders think; they feel their future may depend on making a positive impression on them. But ultimately, psychological safety is built by everyone— at all levels of the company.

In organization after organization that we have studied, psychological safety varies substantially across groups—even when the organization has a strong corporate culture overall. Some groups have healthy learning environments, and others are crippled by interpersonal fear. (For example, one CFO we know didn't speak up with concerns about a planned merger because he was reluctant to be "the skunk at the picnic." He deeply regretted his silence later when the merger failed—at great cost to the company.) The variance tells us that psychological safety is local.

Yes, it's both powerful and helpful when senior executives in a company strike a sincere tone of humility and curiosity, conveying that they understand their dependence on others' input. But it's possible to create a motivated, psychologically safe, high-performing team anywhere. Start by focusing on your own team.

In small but important ways, everyone influences the environment. Anyone can call attention to the need for input or ask questions to draw others out, and anyone can respond to others in productive rather than punitive ways. By showing interest in other people's ideas and concerns, team members can reinforce their peers' voices and help establish a productive learning climate. (See "How the Best Teams Keep Good Ideas Alive," HBR.org, May 18, 2022.)

A Road Map for the Journey Ahead

Equipped with an accurate understanding of what psychological safety truly is, you can employ a few simple practices to help build and reinforce it.

Double down on work goals and why they matter

Putting the focus where it belongs—on the critical goals of the team or organization and the reasons they're important—gets people on the same page. Keep in mind that psychological safety is not the end goal; it's merely an enabler of success. Start by asking questions such as, "What do customers (internal or external) need from us? What will it take to deliver that?" Ironically, talking less about psychological safety and more about the goal and the context and why everyone's input matters is the first step in building psychological safety.

Anouk, a consultant, understood this when she helped leaders of a midsize tech company shift their focus from creating psychological safety (the job for which she was hired) to becoming an effective leadership team in a demanding market. Once they made that shift, psychological safety (measured by an online survey) improved. When they had been focused on psychological safety, they had felt they were supposed to be "really nice to one another," which got in the way of having candid conversations.

Calling attention to what your team is trying to achieve may seem pretty basic. It is. But it's also psychologically powerful. An ambitious goal, conveyed in a way that reminds people *why* it matters, makes it easier for team members to take interpersonal risks by reporting bad news or expressing a dissenting view. Years ago, as a new assistant professor at Harvard Business School, one of us (Amy) experienced this directly. Kim Clark, the school's dean at the time, opened each faculty meeting by stating the school's mission (to educate leaders who make a difference in the world). Initially she thought, *Don't we all already know the mission?* Then she noticed how his simple reminder made it easier to take intellectual risks, try new things, and overcome the frequent setbacks that came with mastering research and case-method teaching.

Good leaders build psychological safety by talking about the challenges their organization faces or the goals they want it to achieve. When Cindy Rose took over as president of Microsoft

Western Europe in 2020, she found a team in need of a refresh. Wisely choosing to shift the culture through engaging in the work in a new way, she leaned into CEO Satya Nadella's mission "to empower every person and every organization on the planet to achieve more." She encouraged her team to become obsessed with listening to customers and delivering products they loved and needed. One team member said Rose had a way of "elevating team ambitions" by focusing "on impact versus activity." With an explicit focus on solving customer problems, the team members could appreciate the need for fast, honest reporting of information from the field, sharing new ideas, and seeking help from one another. In short, they felt empowered to speak up—to have more honest and direct conversations.

Improve the quality of team conversations

Once everyone is on the same page about goals or purpose, the real work can start. Whether spoken, written, synchronous, or asynchronous, conversations are how a lot of work gets done. They're how team members coordinate, make decisions, provide performance feedback, shift course, and celebrate a job well done. It is not a stretch to say that the quality of our conversations determines the quality of our results.

The best way to strengthen psychological safety is to lead conversations in a way that encourages information to be shared candidly and processed thoughtfully. That entails asking good questions, listening intently, and pushing for closure. High-quality conversations are both an outcome and a driver of psychological safety. They foster mutual understanding and progress—and create a learning environment as a by-product. They do not necessarily take longer than low-quality conversations. In fact, many low-quality discussions are indirect, repetitive, and frustratingly inefficient. One marker of quality is making progress while using time well.

Unfortunately, many work conversations—whether for coordination, decision-making, or mentoring—fall short of the mark. Relevant information isn't shared, advocacy and updates drive out inquiry and exploration, and progress is limited. Changing this pattern takes skill and practice, but the effort is worth it: People will walk away from conversations feeling energized— more informed, more aligned, more aware of what needs to be done, and better equipped to do their jobs. People will also discover through direct experience that their fears of negative repercussions for candor were unfounded.

Leaders need to be the architects of high-quality conversations. Here are two examples: At one global retailer not known for psychological safety, a senior operations executive decided to focus on improving the culture of his own team. He set up specific meetings that would be "slower than the rhythm of the business," and he asked Neil, a consultant, to help team members hold constructive conversations where they asked one another for help, practiced curiosity, and had discussions that went beyond the usual performance updates. Essentially, they created a micro-climate of psychological safety that allowed the team to perform well. They didn't wait for the whole company to change its culture. At another company a leader was concerned that his team was "too polite." With Anouk's help, he set up a "gloves off" meeting to practice speaking with candor. He wanted, in his words, "no holding back; everybody is to speak their truth without fear of consequence." In both examples the leaders explicitly asked their teams to have a new kind of conversation. Doing so helped both teams make progress on their operational goals. This is how psychological safety is built, interaction by interaction.

Is your team having a high-quality conversation?

To determine whether it is, try employing a simple scale—such as one to five or low, medium, and high—to answer the questions below. You can use the examples of positive and negative behaviors to guide your ratings. Then review your responses to identify potential pitfalls and spark a dialogue on how to overcome them.

Attribute	Self-assessment questions	What to watch for
People are contributing and listening	• Are people sharing information and opinions candidly? • To what extent do people seem to be holding back and saying only safe things?	**Positive:** Everyone appears engaged in the substance of the discussion. **Negative:** One person or a few people dominate the conversation.
Advocacy and inquiry are both present	• What's the balance between advocacy (to promote certain ideas) and inquiry (to understand them)? • Are people asking genuine questions that prompt others to respond with their ideas and concerns?	**Positive:** Good questions are frequent and expand understanding. **Negative:** People get stuck trying to prove their original points, regardless of new information.
Mutual learning and progress are happening	• Do I feel that I am gaining understanding of the topic as the conversation goes on? • Does the team seem closer to making a good decision?	**Positive:** The conversation is disciplined, systematic, and data-driven. **Negative:** The conversation goes around in circles.

We have created a simple and practical framework for assessing the quality of a work conversation. (See the exhibit "Is your team having a high-quality conversation?") People can readily assess—while a conversation is underway—a group's performance along three dimensions: the degree to which people are listening and sharing, the presence of both advocacy and inquiry, and the degree of progress made. If they pay attention to the dynamics taking place, they can correct course as needed. For instance, if you are (or others seem to be) holding back relevant ideas or concerns or feel disengaged, consider pausing to reset. If inquiry is limited, it's time to insert a good question, such as, "What are we missing? What are you hearing from customers? Who has a different view? If this decision backfired, what would turn out to be the reason?" Finally, if the team doesn't seem to be making progress, ask if others think it's struggling too and then work together to get back on track. High-quality conversation is a team sport; it helps when all are willing to do their part to help the team perform.

Institute structures for sharing reflections and tracking progress

Psychological safety is reinforced by structures and rituals that prompt teams to talk about their progress. We don't believe there is one best way to do this; any number of approaches can work. What matters is the discipline of offering honest appraisals of what's going on with the work (performance against goals) and of the team climate and quality of interactions.

We studied PepsiCo UK a few years ago when it adopted new team practices, including a commitment to discussing work results, insights, and learnings at the end of each week. These progress reports avoided "the big reveal" trap, where people wait until they believe the work is good enough to be shared only to discover that what was produced didn't fit colleagues' expectations or assumptions. Sharing incomplete and imperfect output reduced wasted effort—and allowed better coordination and progress.

Rose at Microsoft instituted a weekly "office hours" virtual meeting for people to drop in and discuss whatever was on their minds. She also launched after-action reviews in which the team dug in to discover lessons following a disappointing business result or client interaction. These sessions were playfully dubbed "failure parties." Inspired by them, the leader of one of the country business units put up a "failure wall" to encourage people to share and learn from stories about taking intelligent risks that didn't pan out. Structured rituals for reflection like these helped psychological safety deepen and spread.

Sometimes reflection processes cross teams. A sales leader at an insurance company was frustrated with the interactions between his people and the compliance team, so he reached out to its leader to suggest reviewing how they could support each other. The two designed a new process that included regular meetings between the leaders to keep the teams aligned and asking team members to reach out to one another directly instead of going through the leaders. The result, according to the sales leader, was that "life got easier for everyone." Work was completed faster, and overtime was reduced.

. . .

Common misconceptions about psychological safety are impeding organizations' performance. In fact, these misunderstandings have led some to dismiss psychological safety as a passing management fad. Yet a deeper understanding of the concept suggests that the need for psychological safety is here to stay. Creating it may not be easy, and practicing it may not be comfortable. But the pace of change and the level of uncertainty in the business environment make frank, data-driven conversations more valuable than ever.

Timely input, candid feedback, and robust debate are as vital for ensuring innovation as for preventing strategic blunders. Leaders who create the kinds of teams that practice these ways of interacting will be poised to outperform those who do not. Ultimately, psychological safety is about changing the expectations for how we work together to successfully navigate the storms ahead.

Originally published in May–June 2025. Reprint R2503D

What's the Best Way to Communicate on a Global Team?

by Dan Bullock and Raúl Sánchez

L anguage is complex and ever evolving. It comes with slang, idioms, and jargon—all of which are culturally specific and may be interpreted in various ways by different people. Accurately representing our thoughts, feelings, and ideas through words is a challenge that every one of us, in every industry, faces.

As remote work-from-anywhere opportunities grow, more and more people will be interacting on global teams. Forging relationships and clearly communicating with people from diverse backgrounds, located in diverse areas of the world, requires a more intentional effort.

Though English is often referred to as the lingua franca (or common language) of the international workforce—spoken by nearly 1.75 billion people—it's not always straightforward. Like most languages, it has several variants, depending on geography, community, and culture.

In the United States, for instance, people use idioms (such as "off the cuff") and sports references (like "home run") when chatting on the job. In India, you'll often hear English phrases that are literal translations from Hindi (such as "do one thing"), and in Australia, slang and abbreviations are commonplace (for example, "Did you watch footy on the telly?").

These expressions, easily understood domestically, are often too exclusive to resonate across cultures, and can lead to break-downs in communication on multinational teams. But there may be a solution: a variant of the English language called *Global English*, which has been linked to a company's ability to innovate globally.

What Is Global English?

It's a type of English focused on clarity, with a limited number of idioms and cultural references. Simply put, it's a style of written and spoken English that's been optimized for clearer and more accurate communication on global teams.

The Global English approach is similar to using "plain lan-guage," or jargon-free language. For example, instead of saying "we need their *buy-in*," you could say "we need their *support*." However, Global English goes one step further than plain lan-guage by including cultural nuances, such as etiquette.

As faculty members at New York University and language and communications specialists at the United Nations Headquar-ters, we train students and professionals to communicate more effectively across intercultural environments. This includes using Global English to successfully manage a project, send an important email, or negotiate across cultures. We have learned

Idea in Brief

The Problem

English is often referred to as the lingua franca (or common language) of multinational teams. But it has its challenges. Culturally specific language—such as slang, idioms, jargon, and acronyms—is common in the workplace, but using it can lead to breakdowns in communication.

The Solution

Global English is a style of written and spoken English that's been optimized for clearer and more accurate communication on multinational teams. To successfully adopt it:

1. Choose clarity over business speak, and replace jargon with literal words.

2. Ditch abbreviations, which can be confusing if you're not in the know.

3. Use cultural references only in domestic settings, where they'll be easily understood, and use more direct language globally.

4. Connect with empathy, but forgo humor—it may not translate across cultures.

that, through Global English, we can foster both greater human understanding and more innovation.

Based on our experience, here are some linguistic strategies to optimize your English and connect more clearly with your global teammates, colleagues, or clients. This will not only help you accomplish your goals, but, importantly, it will create more inclusive environments by allowing you to connect with others—no matter where you, or they, are located.

Choose clarity over "business speak"

It's tempting to recycle business-isms you might hear from your manager or teammates, such as "this has lots of moving parts" or "let's put out some feelers." This is especially true when you've just joined a new team or organization and you feel you need to adopt the common language to connect with others through chitchat. That may be the case in a domestic work environment—but in a multinational office, those phrases just sound like industry jargon. (In fact, recent research indicates that recent graduates and early-career professionals tend to use "business speak" to build rapport with colleagues at work, while Global English is more often used to forge international connections.[1])

If you are entering (or reentering) the global workforce, be mindful of business speak and idioms—phrases with a cultural meaning separate from the literal definition of the individual words, such as "off the top of my head," "cut and dry," and "go the extra mile."[2] Instead, the next time you craft a message to one of your teammates, replace business-isms and idioms with literal words, or add background details when jargon references are inevitable. For example, simplify the phrase "key takeaways" by saying "important points," replace "pain points" with "challenges," and swap "paradigm shift" with "significant change."

Ditch abbreviations

If you end up working on a global team—especially in a government organization—you will likely find that people use multiple abbreviations. These are meant to be shortcuts to effective communication, but, more often, they resemble an insider's code. In any industry, even though our busy work lives encourage us to favor brevity over clarity, you should pay attention to how many abbreviations you use. When people are communicating in global teams, abbreviations can seem like a nonsensical string of letters to anyone outside of your domestic organization. In fact, global heads of training have pointed out that shortcuts such as "OOO" and "ETA" are often baffling and can be misinterpreted.[3]

Additional confusion may result from some abbreviations in British English being different from American English.

Watch out for two kinds of abbreviations: *initialisms* and *acronyms*. In any field, you will be sure to encounter *initialisms*, such as "B2B" and "KPIs" (short for "business to business" and "key performance indicators"), where every character is pronounced separately. Conversely, *acronyms* such as "NATO" (short for North Atlantic Treaty Organization) are pronounced as words and tend to reference initiatives, agencies, or policies. Acronyms are also common in social media (think "YOLO," which stands for "you only live once"). Generally, when writing to global team members, the best practice is to employ the full wording for the first use (with the abbreviation in parentheses) before using the abbreviation on its own. When speaking to global teams, state the abbreviation first, followed by a brief explanation of the full wording. No matter the industry, keep both initialisms and acronyms consistent—but use them sparingly.

Use familiar language domestically and literal language globally

Colorful phrases and witty cultural references can make content more relatable to domestic audiences—and you may use it because you hear your seniors use them—but literal language is preferred when communicating in a multinational office or with team members located globally. One typical pitfall is the *phrasal verb*. These two- or three-word idiomatic expressions ("get ahead," "zero in on," "barrack for") are tricky when speaking to global teams because these verb phrases have a different meaning than the definition of each word.

Our advice? Use a single-word verb instead of a phrasal verb. For example, ditch the verb phrase "firm up" and use "finalize," or replace the verb phrase "draw up" (for a document) with "draft," "write," or "formulate." If you're using pronouns (he, she, they, etc.), make sure to use the person's name first, as some languages don't use pronouns to replace names.

Finally, selectively use culturally centered expressions or references when speaking with colleagues on your team. American culture, for example, is littered with phrases referencing baseball, such as "out of left field" and "you're on deck." Many business expressions around the world also have their origins in Greek mythology, such as "Herculean task" and "the Midas touch"—references not everyone will understand. A culturally-centered expression may help you build rapport in a particular situation, but only use pop-culture examples from advertising, film, and other media (such as "follow the yellow brick road") when you're sure these references are known by all of your team members.

Connect with empathy instead of humor

Similar to catchy idioms, we often use humor as an easy way to connect with coworkers. Yet when we tell jokes in a global team, we may risk appearing insensitive. In Global English, one example is to avoid sarcastic humor, as it involves saying the exact opposite of what we mean. Playful expressions such as "Beautiful day, isn't it?" when it's pouring rain and "Well, that's just what we need" when the situation clearly isn't positive may not connect with global team members, regardless of the good-natured intent.

Instead, use the positive language of *empathy*, such as personal pronouns—*we* and *us*—to connect with colleagues globally and to create inclusion. Also, instead of using playful sarcasm to poke fun at a situation, use optimism to express rational hopes about the future. Highlighting shared commonalities and goals will produce more collaborative and meaningful interactions—and will likely leave an inspiring and lasting impression.

So the next time you present to your international coworkers, email a partner in another part of the world, or negotiate with people across cultures, look up at the International Space Station orbiting in the night sky and remember that it's there because the greatest minds from around the world were able to communicate and execute their ideas. Effective global communication can lead the world to innovation. Global English has the potential to unite continents in creativity and human understanding as business continues to progress rapidly toward a more diverse and global workforce. You can help lead that change.

Adapted from hbr.org, March 22, 2021.

8

Are You Really a Good Listener?

by Jeffrey Yip and Colin M. Fisher

A mple research has shown that when people believe that their managers and senior leaders are truly listening to their ideas and concerns, work relationships grow stronger, engagement rises, and performance improves. That's why bosses have regular one-on-ones with their direct reports, new division heads go on listening tours, and CEOs host all-staff meetings and town halls.

However, studies also show that such practices often are ineffective—in part because many managers simply aren't good listeners. When we conducted a comprehensive review of 117 academic papers on workplace listening—whether it happened in individual conversations or in team or larger meetings—we found that this skill is far easier to describe than to display.[1]

Why? Because listening is an intentional activity that requires empathy, patience, and the ability to respond to what you hear. And because it can be so mentally taxing, particularly when the subject matter is complex or emotionally charged, people often take shortcuts or disengage altogether.

Take Google's all-company TGIF meetings. For years these were biweekly open forums where company leaders would share updates, discuss strategic developments, and take questions from employees. They played a critical role in maintaining a culture of trust at the company.[2] As Laszlo Bock, Google's former senior vice president of people operations, once explained, they covered "everything from whether the mix of food in the cafés is too healthy to really sublime questions around whether our strategy with a particular country or product is good or evil."[3] However, in 2019 Sundar Pichai, Google's CEO, decided that the meetings were no longer working.[4] Employees wanted to talk about contentious issues like the company's handling of hate speech and sexual harassment, and discussions were often leaked to the press.[5] Pichai made them less regular and changed their format. It seems that listening to everyone had gotten too difficult.

Similar scenarios have played out at Activision Blizzard, where an attempt to address harassment claims during a company town hall led to a massive walkout, with workers complaining that leaders were minimizing rather than meaningfully addressing their concerns, and at Amazon, where employees said that a daily survey designed to gauge their sentiment was being skewed by managers' overt pressure to give positive answers and by worries that responses wouldn't be kept anonymous.[6]

In our research we've found that even the most well-intentioned leaders are sometimes guilty of being poor listeners. We've identified five of the most common and damaging causes of that failure: haste, defensiveness, invisibility, exhaustion, and inaction. In this article we'll explain how to avoid those pitfalls and become the kind of listener that your team members need you to be.

Idea in Brief

The Problem

Research has shown that when employees feel heard, their engagement rises and their performance improves, delivering big benefits to their firms. Yet 117 studies on workplace listening reveal that many managers aren't good listeners. Why? Because listening is mentally taxing and demands empathy and patience.

The Solution

The authors explain the five common causes of poor listening and how to counter each.

- **Haste.** To avoid the first pitfall, set aside distraction-free time for conversations, ask clarifying questions, seek more details, and plan follow-up discussions.
- **Defensiveness.** When you get defensive, calm your emotions, buy yourself time by restating what you've heard, and get more information before responding.
- **Invisibility,** or not showing that you're listening. Demonstrate that you are listening with body language and verbal cues and by summarizing what people have told you.
- **Exhaustion,** which can prevent leaders from engaging productively. Setting clear boundaries and acknowledging your limits will help you address this problem.
- **Inaction.** The fix for the final pitfall is to always close the loop: Before ending a conversation, affirm what you've heard, identify next steps, and agree on a timeline for checking back in.

1. Haste

In April 2023 MillerKnoll's CEO, Andi Owen, held an online town hall. Going in, she worried that morale was low. In order for the employees—including her—to receive their annual bonuses, the company needed to hit a revenue goal, and sales weren't on track. But Owen believed that with a final push the employees could succeed. "My goal was to get them to . . . say, 'Gosh, it really stinks that we aren't further along.' And maybe take a minute and feel bad about that, but then sort of leave that place of feeling bad. We still have a quarter, we can still do this," she later told *Fast Company*.[7]

Toward the end of the meeting, Owen was asked the question on everyone's mind: What about the bonuses? And that's when things went awry. "Don't ask about, 'What are we going to do if we don't get a bonus?'" Owen replied. Workers should focus instead on making their numbers, she said, adding: "I had an old boss who said to me one time, 'You can visit pity city, but you can't live there.' So people, leave pity city!" A video of the response went viral, racking up nearly 6 million views and igniting a firestorm online.

Owen had fallen prey to haste. Her viral comment came in the final moments of a long meeting. She hadn't left much time for questions or formulated any responses in advance—so she responded quickly. That often happens with busy leaders managing several people or entire teams.

But listening with haste can be worse than not listening at all. When you respond to people too quickly, they're likely to feel frustrated, demeaned, or unimportant. And when you miss the message because you're hurrying, you may also make decisions based on incomplete information, which can further demotivate your team.

Good listening is a demanding task that takes time. In our work we've found that people feel heard only when listeners focus their attention, demonstrate interest, and ensure that they've understood.

To avoid hasty responses, set aside adequate, distraction-free time for conversations. This signals that you're genuinely invested in hearing the other person's perspective and helps ensure that nothing important gets glossed over. If there are issues you can't address in the moment, plan another time to follow up.

Though this approach may not apply in situations where you're confronted, as Owen was, there are other ways to slow down and listen effectively. One good strategy is to ask clarifying questions. Exploring areas of ambiguity or seeking additional details will not only help you fully understand what you're being told but also encourage people to be more thorough and transparent with you—because you're showing that you truly care about what they're saying.

Finally, resist the urge to interrupt. Research, including a study from Italy's Second University of Naples, shows that interruptions are almost always poorly received.[8] Your first job is to understand the message and intent of the speaker. Respond only after that job is done.

2. Defensiveness

When employees raise concerns or offer critical feedback, defensiveness can be a natural, knee-jerk reaction. For instance, James Clarke, the CEO of Clearlink, reportedly became defensive when responding to complaints about the company's return-to-office policy, which abruptly required all employees within 50 miles of headquarters to work on-site four days a week.[9] Many people were surprised and upset, but instead of listening to them, Clarke lashed out, questioning the motives of those who disagreed with the policy, expressing doubt that working mothers could be productive, and—bizarrely—praising an employee who sold the family dog so that she could comply with the policy.

A similar pattern can be seen in Owen's response. Instead of validating employees' worries, she responded defensively, telling people not to ask the question. Pichai's shift to TGIF meetings that focus on product and business strategy rather than other issues also reflects defensiveness.

Such reactions are not just unproductive; they erode trust and morale. Employees who feel dismissed are more likely to disengage, which weakens relationships and leads to poor organizational outcomes. By contrast, when listeners avoid being judgmental and instead express empathy, speakers are less anxious and thus better able to handle disagreement should it arise, according to research from Guy Itzchakov, Avraham Kluger, and Dotan Castro.[10]

The lesson is to steel yourself against defensiveness by calming your own emotions and seeking to understand the other parties' intentions before responding. Before you speak, take stock of yourself. If you feel criticized or threatened, buy yourself time by simply restating what you think the speaker has said or thanking that person for sharing. You can also ask questions to get more information. Those moves will prevent you from counterattacking and show people that you're hearing them out before voicing your own opinion.

3. Invisibility

One of the most common mistakes we see among managers is not showing that they're listening, which makes them appear indifferent and disconnected. Sometimes organizational leaders are working behind the scenes to fix problems identified in town halls or staff surveys but fail to broadcast those efforts to employees. Or managers are indeed hearing and understanding their employees but not providing any visible signs of engagement.

At Google, for example, Pichai hasn't stopped listening to employees or working to fix problems they raise—he is by most accounts a caring and attentive leader. But by changing the TGIF meetings, he removed a very visible symbol of his willingness to hear feedback. Consider, too, the famous moment during the 1992 U.S. presidential debate, when George Bush Sr., running for reelection, checked his wristwatch just before a voter asked him a question about the national debt and the recession. His response—"Of course, you feel it when you're president of the United States; that's why I'm trying to do something about it, by stimulating the export, investing more, a better education system"—was overshadowed by the gesture, which many perceived as a signal he was ready for the town hall to be over.

To avoid appearing indifferent, leaders must be more communicative and transparent. They can use body language known as "back channeling"—behaviors that signal that they're listening. They include maintaining eye contact, nodding, and adopting an open posture (with your arms relaxed at your sides rather than crossed in front of your chest, for example). Research by Janet Bavelas and colleagues shows that such cues make conversations more productive: When a listener signals comprehension, it allows the speaker to move on; when a listener shows confusion, it invites the speaker to rephrase or elaborate.[11]

Verbal acknowledgments are important too. Simple phrases such as "I see" or "That makes sense" signal to your counterparts that you're following along, valuing their perspective, and actively processing their messages.

Finally, you can demonstrate listening by reflecting the ideas of speakers back to them. Summarizing what you've heard is a powerful way to confirm your understanding. For example, you might say, "So what I'm hearing is that you're concerned about the deadline because it might not allow enough time for testing." This approach not only reassures the speaker that you're attentive but helps prevent any misunderstandings. C-suite leaders can also use it in emails or other corporate communications after receiving employee survey results or after all-staff meetings.

4. Exhaustion

Exhaustion is a silent killer of effective listening. When leaders are physically or emotionally drained, they lose their capacity to focus, process, and engage productively with employees. Imagine a boss who has just finished back-to-back meetings and skipped lunch and is now on a late-afternoon call with a team member sharing a pressing concern. Despite being present physically, her attention drifts, and she's unable to respond thoughtfully.

That's probably how Google leaders felt as one TGIF meeting after another surfaced a slew of difficult employee concerns. At a small startup, a weekly meeting that allows all employees to talk to top management is realistic. At a company of 100,000, it's more difficult. Similarly, Owen, Clarke, and Bush Sr. were no doubt tired—from managing their organizations and the country, respectively—when they made their listening gaffes.

According to research by Christopher Rosen and colleagues, managers who listen to too many complaints eventually become so worn down that they're more likely to mistreat their subordinates.[12]

The best way to avoid exhausted listening is to establish clear boundaries. That might involve blocking out certain hours when your door or calendar is open and others when it's not, setting time limits on discussions, or taking breaks during extended conversations.

Moreover, leaders should acknowledge their personal limits. If you're feeling weary, it's both acceptable and beneficial to reschedule for a time when you have more energy. By acknowledging that quality listening requires mental and emotional reserves, you're demonstrating transparency and respect, which your counterparts will appreciate.

Remember, too, that it's OK to ask for help. While listening to employee problems and concerns is an essential part of a leader's job, it can be shared. Too often, one manager becomes the office therapist everyone turns to for venting and advice. In such cases the overburdened manager can ask colleagues and team members to check in with their employees and peers to share the listening load. If your organization has regular meetings like TGIFs where people voice suggestions and concerns, the person running them should rotate. That will help prevent individuals from being overwhelmed and foster a sense of collective responsibility.

5. Inaction

The final pitfall is perhaps the most pernicious: receiving the speaker's message but then not following up on it. Google's slow response to employee concerns about sexual harassment in 2018, for instance, led 20,000 employees to walk out—and contributed to increasingly contentious TGIF meetings.[13]

Research backs up the idea that inaction after employees raise issues erodes trust between managers and subordinates. In one study, Michaela Kerrissey and colleagues interviewed nurses during the Covid-19 pandemic; many reported feeling "unheard, frustrated, and alienated from their managers" because nothing had come of numerous meetings with them to discuss concerns.[14]

. . .

Listening without subsequent action or explanation leads employees to believe their efforts—and yours—have been pointless. There is a fix for this: Always close the loop. Before ending a conversation, affirm what you've heard, identify the next steps for action, and agree on a timeline for checking back in. That emphasizes forward momentum and ensures accountability.

Be transparent about what you can or cannot act on, and in all cases explain why. If you're taking an employee's suggestion, outline how you want the team to make it happen. If a requested change can't be implemented because of budget constraints, company policy, or other limitations, acknowledge that reality. Delineating the reasons behind inaction can open the door to brainstorming alternative approaches.

Listening is a cognitively and emotionally demanding activity. It takes deliberate attention and effort to avoid the five pitfalls we've described here. But if you master this managerial skill, you will build stronger relationships, foster greater trust, minimize misunderstandings, and create opportunities for meaningful change. Don't let haste, defensiveness, invisibility, exhaustion, and inaction keep you from becoming a better listener and leader.

Originally published in May–June 2025. Reprint R2503N

9

What People Still Get Wrong About Negotiations

by Max H. Bazerman

One of the simulations I use when teaching managers to negotiate more effectively involves a technology transfer between two divisions of a corporation. The price of the transfer is central to the negotiation, but there are other important issues to be considered as well. The structure of the deal will affect how much profitability the technology transfer creates for each division and for the company as a whole.

Even when running this simulation with seasoned executives, I am continually struck by the degree to which they fail to reach an agreement that maximizes total profitability. During the debriefing, each side compares the estimated profit it would

---

Editor's note: Max H. Bazerman is the author of *Negotiation: The Game Has Changed* (Princeton University Press, 2025), from which this article is adapted.

accrue in the deal against what the simulation shows it could have obtained. Had the two divisions made wise trades across the various issues rather than simply compromising on each one, both would have ended up with more profit. But most negotiators don't do that. Instead, in effect, they throw corporate cash in the garbage can and burn it.

The question is: Why?

There are two main reasons. First, many executives mistakenly believe that they're negotiating over a fixed pie and that gains for one side necessarily mean losses for the other. Second, they focus exclusively on how to claim value for themselves (by taking as much as they can of that mythical fixed pie) rather than coming up with ways to increase the size of the pie.

The simple genius of value creation in negotiation is that everybody benefits. That principle is not new, but I find that people at all managerial levels have lost sight of it and urgently need to be reminded. In our political, social, personal, and professional lives, we've become more polarized and intransigent than ever. We're less willing and able to see our counterpart's point of view. We're less inclined to engage in problem-solving, and without the understanding that comes from that process, we have trouble finding mutually beneficial deals. As the policy expert Heather McGhee explains in *The Sum of Us*, we routinely forgo the "solidarity dividend"—the gains we could achieve from working productively across boundaries to accomplish what we can't do on our own. In short, despite what we've learned over the years, we keep getting negotiation wrong.

Over my career I've taught tens of thousands of MBA and executive-education students the principles of good negotiation, and I've always tried to instill in them the importance of value creation. Value creators, the evidence plainly shows, are more

The Problem

Most executives leave value on the negotiating table, for two main reasons: They assume they're negotiating over a fixed pie, and they focus exclusively on how to claim value from that pie for themselves.

The Approach

To create value and reach efficient agreements, negotiators should choose from four strategies: Build trust and share information, ask questions, give away some information, and make multiple offers.

The Wrap-Up

As a final step, consider meeting one more time after the deal has been signed, when people are likely to feel less adversarial, to see if there are additional terms that might make the deal better for everyone.

effective negotiators, develop stronger relationships, have better reputations—and, dare I say it, contribute to making the world a better place.

In this article I lay out negotiation strategies that can help you become the best value creator possible.

Preparing for Value-Creating Negotiations

Before entering into a negotiation, it's important to think through all the issues that you and your counterpart might care about. Suppose a VC firm is negotiating terms for a $2 million investment in a startup. Although the main issue on the table is the percentage of equity that the VC firm will receive, both sides should think in advance about other factors that affect the attractiveness of various deal options. These might include the value or cost of a board seat, the value or cost of consulting advice from the VC firm, options for additional equity in the future, and so on. The goal is not to create unneeded complexity but to foster the conditions for crafting an agreement that is better for both parties than what they might arrive at simply by haggling over the equity percentage. (For more on this topic, see Deepak Malhotra's May 2013 HBR article "How to Negotiate with VCs.")

Once you've identified a broad list of issues, the next step is to determine their relative importance. Every multi-issue negotiation will require you to make trade-offs, explicitly or implicitly. If you are the VC firm, how much equity are you willing to give up to secure a consulting contract with the startup? How much would you give up for a board seat? Such calculations can be difficult, often involving what feel like apples-to-oranges comparisons. If you rely on intuition to make those trades on the spot—rather than consider in advance how many oranges you would give up for 10 apples—you're likely to leave value on the table.

In my simulations, I often provide participants with a description of the range of issues at hand and a score sheet that weights each according to its importance. The metric might be in dollars or points. Scoring systems help participants evaluate package offers from the other party and structure their own offers strategically. In the weighting process, they usually find that some issues matter greatly to them but don't matter much or at all to the other side. It's critical to identify those issues.

Say you're negotiating a job offer. You may be indifferent about whether you start your new job in June or July. But if your potential employer strongly prefers that you start as soon as possible, you're positioned to give it something it values at no cost to you and get something of value in return (such as a preferred initial project). Or imagine that you're buying a house, and your mortgage is secured. A contractor friend looks the place over before you submit an offer and confirms that the house doesn't have

Using a Weighted Score Sheet to Evaluate Multiple Offers

To compare deal options in multi-issue negotiations, I recommend using a score sheet—as a graduating student and I did recently when she stopped by my office for advice on negotiating two job offers. She had an offer in hand from Firm A for a position based in Chicago with a salary of $200,000. The job had a July 1 start date and no starting bonus. She expected to receive an offer from Firm B within 48 hours. Together, we created a weighted score sheet for evaluating the second offer, allotting dollar values to her preferences for one firm over the other, the job location, the start date, and a starting bonus. If the total value to her of Firm B's offer were to be higher than $200,000, she would be wise to accept it.

A score sheet can be used to test a range of hypothetical offers—a useful exercise that will help you think clearly about your options before you experience the rush of emotion that we all feel when presented with high-stakes offers.

Offer from Firm B

Salary	$
Attractiveness of Firm B relative to Firm A	+$20,000
Job location	$
Chicago: no adjustment	
San Francisco: +$20,000	
Dallas: -$12,000	
Start date	$
7/1/25: no adjustment	
6/1/25: -$5,000	
8/1/25: +$10,000	
Starting bonus (multiply one-time bonus by .3)	$
Total	$

any major problems. You are positioned to make your offer on the house without an inspection or mortgage contingencies. This concession costs you little, but it might be of significant value to a seller who wants assurance that the sale will go through. It might also make your offer more attractive than those of other bidders.

Many executives I work with point out that no actual negotiation comes with a weighted score sheet. That has been my experience too. When I ask them whether such a tool might be helpful, I see a light bulb go on in their heads: *We need to do this*. (See the sidebar "Using a Weighted Score Sheet to Evaluate Multiple Offers.")

Strategies for Value Creation at the Table

I often ask experienced executives whether they think it's best to start with the easy issues in a complex negotiation or the tough ones. Many respond that the easy ones should be tackled first. They argue that this allows negotiators on both sides to build trust and gather momentum. If you start with a difficult issue, they say, you might derail the negotiation from the start. Other executives argue that it's better to begin with the tough issues. If you can't reach agreement on those, they say, there's no point in wasting time on less important things. Just move on to an alternative buyer or supplier. A third group says simply, "It depends."

All three groups are wrong. That's because I've asked a trick question: *No* issue should be resolved first. Any process that negotiates the issues sequentially is a barrier to finding the trades across issues that allow for value creation. This doesn't mean that you need to talk about everything at the same time. But it does mean that you should avoid finalizing an agreement on any one issue before you've had the opportunity to discuss them all. Once you have a better idea of the totality of issues on the table, you can begin exploring relative preferences across issues, finding trades, and creating value. In economics lingo, your goal should be to jointly define the *Pareto-efficient frontier*—that is, the range of options such that there is no option that is better for one or more parties without making another party worse off.

All too often, however, negotiators fail to share information about preferences on the various issues, fearful that they will be exploited if the other side knows what they value. They keep all their cards hidden and assume that this is the secret to being a tough negotiator.

To elicit the information necessary to create value, resolve conflicts, and reach efficient agreements, I recommend four strategies. You should have all of these in your toolbox and know how to select the right one for a given situation.

Strategy 1: Build trust and share information

Imagine you're the CEO in the technology transfer scenario. The two divisions are each rewarded for their own profitability; you and the company's shareholders are affected by the combined profitability across the entire organization. Naturally, you want both divisions to share all their information openly and honestly so that they can make a creative deal that maximizes total profit. Yes, each division will care about how much of the pie it claims for itself, but you don't want that to keep them from figuring out ways to expand the pie.

There is another key issue in the negotiation besides the transfer price: Division A wants to preserve its competitive advantage by keeping the technology out of the hands of its rivals; Division B wants to use the technology in its products to boost sales to customers, including to Division A's rivals. To make the best deal, the divisions need to reveal to each other how much the restriction on selling to competitors would cost Division B and how value would be created for Division A by protecting its technology. Those assessments should dictate what deal creates the most value for the company.

Many executives have told me that they find it tougher to negotiate with people inside their company than with outside suppliers and customers. To me that suggests a big problem. A main responsibility of leaders is to create an organizational culture in which people are trusting, trustworthy, and open about information, including about how much they value the various issues on the table. If you can create a culture of trust, you'll be well positioned to focus on value creation.

In many negotiations, of course, trust between parties isn't strong enough for that kind of openness. But that doesn't mean we should give up the pursuit to create value.

Strategy 2: Ask questions

Part of your job as a negotiator is to learn as much as possible from the other party about what it wants so that you can make an attractive offer that creates ample value for your side. That means acknowledging openly what you don't know—and asking questions. The other party won't always answer them, but it's certainly more likely to share information if you ask than if you don't.

The trick, of course, is knowing how to pose the right question. "Can you just tell me what you really want?" is less likely to lead to useful information than "Can you help me understand how important various issues are to you so that we can put an offer on the table that will be attractive to you?" or "Of all the issues you have mentioned, which is most critical to your team?" or "How much of issue A would you give up for an extra unit of issue B?"

Asking questions is especially important when the other party makes an offer that surprises you or that you're skeptical about. Suppose the VC firm looking to invest in the startup keeps pushing its consulting services in the negotiation. The startup might view this as either unreasonable or a distraction, given that what it cares most about is funding. But an astute negotiator, recognizing that this is valuable information, would probe deeper:

- Can you tell me more about your consulting services and why you think we need them?

- Would you accept contingent payment for the consulting services based on the cost reductions they create?

- Are you willing to accept a lower equity position in the firm if we accept your proposed consulting arrangement?

The VC firm's answers may provide very useful hints about whether the consulting arrangement is likely to add value to the deal.

Strategy 3: Give away some information

What should you do in a negotiation when trust remains low and the other side is not responding to your questions? Consider giving away some information.

Humans tend to reciprocate behavior. If you yell at somebody, that person is likely to yell back. If you apologize, you often get an apology in return. And if you provide useful and honest information to the other side, you are likely to find that your counterpart is more willing to share information with you. That's what's known as the norm of reciprocity in action. It's critical to share the right kinds of information, of course. Rarely should you start by sharing your reservation value (the value of the least favorable deal you'd be willing to accept), because that would only help the other side claim value from you. But once you've jump-started the process by sharing some of your priorities, the flow of information is likely to begin, whether your counterpart is a skilled negotiator or not.

Consider a graduating MBA student who wants to negotiate the location and start date of a job offer. How might she provide information to get the best outcome? Imagine if she said the following: "I hope we can reach a mutually beneficial agreement. I prefer your firm over my other options. But you seem to be leaning toward making me an offer in Chicago, and I would really value spending my first two years in San Francisco, because my partner was just accepted into the MBA program at Berkeley. In addition, my partner and I are getting married in June, and a later start date would allow us to take the honeymoon that we have planned for quite a while." Notice that the candidate has not refused an offer that fails to meet her preferences, but she has opened up a dialogue about her priorities and what the firm might do to make its offer more attractive than the others she is considering.

Strategy 4: Make multiple offers simultaneously

Despite your best efforts, you may find yourself negotiating with opponents who resist sharing information. In those situations, you'll need a tactic that elicits information without the other party's directly providing it.

That brings us to our fourth strategy: Instead of making just one offer at a time, make several at once. The offers should be of equal value to you but differ from one another on the issues at stake. Our VC firm could simply propose a 27% stake in the startup for its investment. But a more fruitful approach might be to simultaneously make three offers that it perceives to be of equal value:

1. a 27% stake for $2 million;

2. a 24% stake for $2 million and a consulting contract for advice on manufacturing and distribution for a fee of $400,000; or

3. a 20% stake for $2 million, free consulting on manufacturing and distribution, and an additional 8% stake if the startup (a) obtains a viable co-manufacturing agreement within 18 months, (b) gets its products in at least 2,000 retail locations within 24 months, and (c) secures at least $2 million in its next round of funding within 30 months.

Note that the last option might ultimately leave the startup with the smallest stake, but that stake would be worth much more overall if all the performance conditions are met.

The ball is now in the startup's court—and its response can be telling. Let's say the startup responds that none of the three offers is entirely acceptable but the third is the best starting point for further discussion. That response reveals where more value can be created and provides the VC firm with information that it might not have gained by asking direct questions. It also signals the firm's willingness to be accommodating and its interest in moving forward in the negotiation.

Note that the startup does not have to accept any of the offers to signal its relative priorities. Its desire to negotiate the third offer puts the VC firm on a path to a value-creating deal, even if it shaves a good number of percentage points off the up-front stake. From there, the VC firm can tailor the deal in a way that continues to expand the pie.

So which of the above negotiation strategies should you start with to create more value? That depends on the context. If you have a great relationship with your counterpart, strategy 1 will be the obvious choice: You share information, turn the negotiation into a problem-solving session, and work together to define the Pareto-efficient frontier. If your relationship is good but not good enough for strategy 1, move on to strategies 2 and 3. In cases where trust is low or the relationship is weak, strategy 4 can help you create value.

It's Not Over Just Because It's Over

There's actually a fifth strategy that I recommend for value creation, but it's one to use after you've reached an agreement.

Many of us have made deals we aren't fully satisfied with—and perhaps the other side isn't either. In such cases, there may still be value left on the table. So why stop just because you've come to an agreement? Why not try to improve the deal with a post-settlement settlement (PSS), an idea first suggested by the decision theorist Howard Raiffa.

Imagine you've just reached an agreement with a tough counterpart and want nothing more than to put the long, difficult negotiation process behind you. Resist that urge. Instead, consider telling the other side that you are committed to implementing the agreement as is, but then note that it might be beneficial to meet one more time to see if terms could be added to make the deal better for both of you. You may find that after shaking hands on the deal or signing the agreement, everybody is feeling less adversarial and more open to sharing information. Be sure to clarify that in proposing a PSS you are not reneging on the deal or looking for additional concessions. Be clear that the initial agreement will remain in place unless you identify additional wise trades and come to a new agreement that creates more value.

And there's no reason you have to negotiate a PSS immediately upon agreeing to your initial deal. It might be best for the two parties to work together for a few weeks to give themselves time to establish trust and better understand each other's interests.

Value Creation as a Way of Life

We all negotiate constantly. I negotiate with my unit head over my teaching assignments. I negotiate with colleagues on who will do what work on a project. I negotiate with consulting clients about the scope of projects and my fees. As a small-stakes investor, I negotiate with startups. I negotiate with my spouse every day.

None of the people I negotiate with would describe me as a pushover. But I hope and expect that they would describe me as a good partner, creative at finding mutually beneficial agreements, and focused on how our agreements affect both of us rather than on whether I "won" or "lost" the negotiation. I do care about claiming a reasonable percentage of the value created for myself, but I find it far easier and more effective to spend more of my efforts on expanding the pie than on claiming it.

And I really don't like waste. In negotiation we waste value when we fail to find mutually beneficial trades. We can, and should, do better. The strategies I've laid out in this article are a great way to start.

Originally published in January–February 2025. Reprint R2501D

10

Cultivating Everyday Courage

by James R. Detert

n many stories we hear about workplace courage, the people who fight for positive change end up being ostracized—and sometimes even lose their jobs. What I've seen in the course of my research, though, tells a more nuanced story. Most acts of courage don't come from whistleblowers or organizational martyrs. Instead, they come from respected insiders at all levels who take action—be it campaigning for a risky strategic move, pushing to change an unfair policy, or speaking out against unethical behavior—because they believe it's the right thing to do. Their reputations and track records enable them to make more headway than those on the margins or outside the organization could. And when they manage the process well, they don't necessarily pay a high price for their actions; indeed, they may see their status rise as they create positive change.

Consider Martha (not her real name), a finance manager at a small company. For years she endured risqué comments and sexual innuendo from her boss, the company president, and she struggled with how to handle it: Should she talk to him about his behavior, or just quit? How could she protect the other women at the firm? Then, at a staff gathering, her boss grabbed her inappropriately during a light moment, thinking it was funny. Later that day, she confronted him in his office, prepared to quit if he made no changes. She told him that his behavior made her uncomfortable and was a signal to her that she'd never advance in the company because he didn't view her as an equal. She said that perhaps he was trying to promote a fun work environment, but he was failing.

Martha was terrified that he would fire her, be angry, or tell her to toughen up. But instead, to her surprise, he apologized. He was horrified that this was how she felt—and that other women in the company probably felt the same way. He praised her for speaking out when no one else had dared to. Over subsequent months, he continued to seek her guidance on the issue and made a formal apology to the staff. A year later, Martha was promoted to a VP role: an incredible position to be in for someone who once believed that the president would never promote a woman to that level.

I began investigating workplace courage after spending more than a decade studying why people so often don't speak up at work. I've found many examples of people at all levels who created positive change without ruining their careers. Their success rested primarily on a set of attitudes and behaviors that can be learned, rather than on innate characteristics. I call people who exhibit these behaviors *competently courageous* because they create the right conditions for action by establishing a strong internal reputation and by improving their fallback options in case things go poorly; they carefully choose their battles, discerning

Idea in Brief

The Challenge

Professionals who perform courageous acts—such as pushing to change a flawed policy or speaking out against unethical behavior—risk their reputations and even their jobs.

A Better Way

People who succeed in their courageous acts, or suffer fewer negative consequences, tend to exhibit certain behaviors and attributes: They lay the groundwork for action; they carefully choose their battles; they manage messaging and emotions; and they follow up afterward.

Getting Started

A good way to learn and master competently courageous behaviors is to engage in smaller, everyday acts before proceeding to progressively more difficult ones. Above all, keep your values and purpose front and center.

whether a given opportunity to act makes sense in light of their values, the timing, and their broader objectives; they maximize the odds of in-the-moment success by managing the messaging and emotions; and they follow up to preserve relationships and marshal commitment. These steps are useful whether you're pushing for major change or trying to address a smaller or more local issue.

Lest anyone think I'm naive, let me be clear: Of course bad things do happen when people challenge authorities, norms, and institutions. Courage, after all, is about taking worthy actions *despite the potential risk*. If no one ever got fired, was socially isolated, or suffered other consequences for a particular action, we wouldn't consider it courageous. And good outcomes are more likely to come from some types of actions than from others. For example, challenging the inappropriate behavior of a colleague with whom you have a decent relationship is, all else being equal, likely to go better for you than defying the entire power structure over an unethical practice.

Among those I studied who had failed to create positive change, almost all still thought their risk-taking had been the right thing to do. They were proud they had stood up for what they believed in—but they wished they'd done so more skillfully. Following the four principles laid out here can help people at all levels improve their chances of creating positive change when they do decide to act.

Laying the Groundwork

My research shows that employees whose workplace courage produces good results have often spent months or years establishing that they excel at their jobs, that they are invested in the organization, and that they're evenhanded. They've demonstrated that they're able to stand both apart from and with those whose support they need. In doing so, they've accumulated what psychologists call idiosyncrasy credits—a stock of goodwill derived from their history of competence and conformity— which they can cash in when challenging norms or those with more power. (I've also seen the reverse: When people with a reputation for selfishness or ill will stand up for legitimately needed change, they tend to be less successful.)

Competently courageous people also work to earn the trust of those who see them as their champions. They invest in those relationships, too—engaging with people individually, taking the time to empathize with them, and helping them develop professionally.

Consider Catherine Gill, a former senior vice president of fundraising and communication at the nonprofit social investment fund Root Capital. Gill wanted to speak up about what she and colleagues saw as the organization's unintentional yet manifest internal bias against women. The issue was particularly tricky because criticizing the leadership could easily be viewed as criticizing the organization's socially conscious mission. But she was able to launch an honest—if painful—conversation with her colleagues in senior management about the organization's culture, leading to a number of concrete changes.

Gill's track record of excelling and fitting in at the organization was fundamental to her success. Over her first two years at Root Capital, she achieved consistently high performance as a fundraiser and exhibited the emotional and intellectual intelligence to navigate complex issues. She showed that she was deeply committed to the organization's mission, regularly adjusting her role to tackle the most pressing challenges and showing how various initiatives she launched were aligned with core strategic priorities. She was careful to point out when she didn't consider something a gender issue so that people on both sides would see her as fair. All that gave her the idiosyncrasy credits she needed to be heard by the leadership team. She determined the limits of what change was possible so that she wouldn't push too far and get "voted off the island." Through her work ethic, judgment, and humor, she set the stage for more visible moments of courageous action.

Sometimes things don't work out, even with the best preparation. Competently courageous people develop mechanisms to mitigate fallout. That might mean finding ways to make themselves indispensable to the organization, keeping external options open, or minimizing economic reliance on an employer. For example, former Telecom Italia leader Franco Bernabè rejected many of the perks that came with being the CEO of a major company, knowing that doing so made it easier to take risks. "If I had lost my job," he said, "and gone back to something more subdued and less glamorous—well, it wouldn't have changed my life."

Choosing Your Battles

Not every opportunity to display courage is worth taking. The people I've studied who have been successful in their courageous acts asked themselves two questions before moving ahead: Is this really important? and, Is this the right time?

Importance, of course, lies in the eye of the beholder. It depends on your goals and values and those of your colleagues, stakeholders, and the organization itself. As you gauge whether an issue is truly important, be aware of your emotional triggers; allow yourself to be informed but not held hostage by them. Also assess whether engaging in a potential battle—whatever the outcome might be—is likely to aid or hinder winning the war. Ask yourself, for example: Will securing resources to address this problem make it less likely that a higher-priority proposal will subsequently get funded?

Competently courageous people are masters of good timing. To avoid being seen as a broken record, they are less likely to act if they recently cashed in hard-earned idiosyncrasy credits. They observe what is going on around them, and if the timing doesn't look right, they patiently hold off. They scan the environment for events and trends that could support their efforts, making the most of an organizational change or the appearance of a new ally, for example. They stay attuned to attention cycles—to public upwellings of enthusiasm for the issue at hand. Pushing for a more globally representative strategy or leadership team, for example, was for a long time risky in many organizations; now companies are more open to tackling those issues.

Unless they've concluded that taking action is necessary to preserve their sense of integrity or to plant the seed of an idea, competently courageous people don't act before those around them are ready to take them seriously.

For example, when "Mandy" joined an accessories and apparel company as a product manager, she quickly learned that one of the company's vendors was highly problematic. Its reps were rude, dishonest, and manipulative, and the product itself was subpar. However, ties between the two companies were long-standing and included a friendship between two key managers. Mandy wisely waited; she didn't suggest a change until six months later. By that point she had demonstrated her commitment to the organization, and she was better able to gauge the relationships between the people involved. She used the intervening time to collect evidence of the problems, identify alternative vendors, and quantify the improvements they could offer. When she finally did make her proposal, the VP in charge responded positively.

In some cases, conditions or events such as sagging sales or a change in leadership create urgency for courageous acts—and make them more likely to succeed. Tachi Yamada, a physician-scientist turned business leader, has been a master of seizing the day during a successful career as a senior executive in the health care sector. When Yamada became head of R&D at SmithKline Beecham in 1999, he quickly concluded that the R&D organization needed to be restructured around disease areas or "assets" (the molecules or compounds that might eventually make it to market) rather than the traditional silos. When a merger with another pharmaceutical giant—Glaxo—was announced, he campaigned for the R&D function of the combined company to be structured in that way. The proposal didn't go over well. R&D leaders and scientists at Glaxo were particularly upset; here was the new guy from the much smaller company in the merger telling them they needed a major change. They "were pretty much aligned against me," recalls Yamada. But he knew that the timing could be used to his advantage: "The merger and the thin pipeline in both companies gave me a burning platform." His push for the reorganization succeeded in part because of his ability to recognize the opportunity and capitalize on it.

Persuading in the Moment

Workplace courage is, of course, about more than preparation. Eventually you must take action. During this step, competently courageous people focus primarily on three things: framing their issue in terms that the audience will relate to, making effective use of data, and managing the emotions in the room. They connect their agenda to the organization's priorities or values, or explain how it addresses critical areas of concern for stakeholders. They ensure that decision makers feel included—not attacked or pushed aside.

Mel Exon, a former executive at the advertising firm Bartle Bogle Hegarty (BBH), excels at framing proposals in ways that make them attractive to those whose support she needs. For example, when Exon and a colleague first pitched the idea for an internal innovation unit—BBH Labs—to senior management, support was far from unanimous. Some executives worried that the creation of a separate innovation group would imply that parts of BBH *weren't* innovative. This was concerning in a firm that proudly considered itself the contrarian visionary in the industry, with a black sheep as its calling card.

To convince the skeptics that BBH Labs was philosophically aligned with the company's mission, Exon took advantage of internal stakeholders' pride in the black sheep image, pointing out that some of BBH's clients had come to the company specifically for groundbreaking ideas. A lab focused on innovation would fulfill exactly that need. She won over others by describing the work of the new lab as advance scouting, promising that everyone at the firm would share in its findings. Exon eventually got the go-ahead from senior management, and later BBH's CEO complimented her approach, describing it as building on the company's DNA rather than trying to change it.

Keeping your cool as you perform your courageous act can be just as important as how you make your case. A manager I'll call Erik, who was tasked with growing the solar business at one of the world's largest multinationals, frequently butted heads with senior executives in the company's traditional lines of business. When he sought their support for new business models, they often pushed back, telling him brusquely, "We don't do that" or "That will never work here." The discussions could get heated, and Erik often felt frustrated by the executives' defensiveness. But instead of taking the emotional bait, he reminded himself that their response was a normal reaction to fear of the unknown. Acknowledging their mindset helped him stay calm and concentrate on simply making data-driven arguments. In the end, he was able to bring others around to his point of view, and the business made a strong pivot toward his recommended strategy.

Following Up

Those who exhibit competent courage follow up after they take action, no matter how things turned out. They manage their relationships with the people involved: When things go well, they thank supporters and share credit. When things go badly, they address lingering emotions and repair ties with those who might be hurt or angry.

For example, Catherine Gill made an in-the-moment decision to launch her campaign to change the culture at Root Capital during a retreat with about 30 leaders present. But as a result of her spontaneous decision, she caught the CEO off guard. Knowing that the very difficult conversation that ensued might have felt to him like an indictment of his leadership—and that he might see her actions as a personal attack—Gill checked in with him privately at that evening's dinner. She assured him that she wasn't trying to start a revolution; she was trying to advance the firm's evolution into its ideal form.

Follow-up also means continuing to pursue your agenda beyond the first big moment of action. Even when their initial steps go well, the competently courageous continue to advocate, reach out to secure resources, and make sure others deliver on promises. And when things don't go well, they take it in stride, viewing setbacks as learning opportunities rather than hiding from the fallout or giving up.

Take Fred Keller, who established a welfare-to-career program at the company he founded, Cascade Engineering. In the initiative's first incarnation, participants were often late or absent, and their performance was poor. Within a few weeks, not one of the new hires remained, and Cascade's employees and supervisors were left feeling frustrated. Instead of giving up, Keller viewed the failure as an opportunity to learn. Finding that neither Cascade nor its new hires had been well prepared for the program, he reinstated it with more training for everyone involved. When this second attempt seemed headed toward a similar fate, Keller harnessed the growing criticism to get it right. He further increased training of leaders and partnered with a county official to bring a social worker on-site to work with the new hires to identify and solve problems before they escalated. This time Keller's persistence and learning paid off: The program is now a core part of the organization and is widely lauded as a model for transitioning people from welfare to work. And through his persistence, Keller earned tremendous loyalty from his staff at all levels of the company.

Getting Started

Courage isn't required only for high-stakes campaigns. My research with Evan Bruno, a PhD student at Darden, shows that a host of everyday actions require employees to act courageously. Sometimes simply doing one's job well requires courage. It's also worth noting that "risk" encompasses more than the prospect of financial ruin or getting fired. Humans naturally fear rejection, embarrassment, and all sorts of other social and economic consequences. From the outside, for example, it might be easy to question whether Fred Keller's actions required courage. As the owner of the company, Keller could do whatever he wanted, so where's the risk? But for years, he faced doubters both inside and outside his organization. To persevere knowing that people might think he was a "nutcase" or that he was wasting time or money took courage.

The good news is that the experiences of those I've studied show that competently courageous behaviors can be learned. They're dependent on effort and practice, rather than on some heroic personality trait limited to the few. (So don't use that as an excuse to let yourself off the hook if you find yourself in a situation that calls for courage!) One piece of advice I give to students and clients: Don't jump into the deep end right away.

Instead, approach this work incrementally by trying smaller, more manageable acts before proceeding to progressively harder ones. That might mean having a difficult conversation in some other sphere of life, or broaching a tough topic with a colleague you like and respect, before confronting a boss about demeaning behavior. It might mean guiding your own team in a new direction before suggesting a transformation of the whole organization. And consider what "small" means to you—we all have different perceptions of which actions require courage. (To see how your perception of what takes courage lines up with others', take our Workplace Courage Acts Index self-assessment at www.workplacecai.com.) Then, as you tackle each step, focus on what you learn, not whether it goes perfectly the first time.

Above all, keep your values and purpose front and center. You'll have a stronger sense of self-respect through any setbacks you face, and you'll be less likely to regret your actions, no matter how things turn out. And by using the principles discussed in this article, you'll increase the chances of successfully creating change, making the risks you take all the more worthwhile.

Originally published in November–December 2018. Reprint R1806K

Discussion Guide

Are you feeling inspired by what you've read in this collection? Do you want to share the ideas in the articles or explore the insights you've gleaned with others? This discussion guide offers an opportunity to dig a little deeper, with questions to prompt personal reflection and to start conversations with your team.

You don't need to have read the book from beginning to end to use this guide. Choose the questions that apply to the articles you have read or that you feel might spark the liveliest discussion.

Reflect on key takeaways from your reading to help you adopt the ideas and techniques you want to integrate into your work as a leader. What tools can you share with your team to help everyone be their best? Becoming the leader you want to be starts with a detailed plan—and a commitment to carrying it out.

1. According to Jay Conger in "The Necessary Art of Persuasion," leaders who hope to persuade others must first establish their credibility. How would you rate your credibility on a scale of 1–10 (1 being the lowest level of credibility and 10 being the highest)? Would your team rate you the same way? What steps could you take to increase your credibility and become more persuasive?

2. How often is your team using questions to spur learning, exchange ideas, and make conversations productive? What groups, processes, or situations would benefit from asking more—and better—questions? How might differing goals for a conversation (building a relationship, accomplishing

something together, or seeking sensitive information, for instance) change the type, tone, and framing of the questions you ask? When would asking more questions *not* be helpful?

3. Describe a recent stressful conversation you had at work with a colleague or client. How did you feel, physically and emotionally? How did you respond—by defending your position or hearing out the other person? Where could you have improved in your discussion, and what habits or strategies can help you stay grounded in future conversations?

4. How do you feel when someone shares emotional or painful information with you—awkward, helpless, anxious, something else? How do you typically respond? In her article "How Supportive Leaders Approach Emotional Conversations," Sarah Noll Wilson identifies some common emotionally dismissive responses. Do you tend to use any of these? How could you be more supportive of others in painful situations?

5. Think of someone whose messages you find particularly compelling, persuasive, or enjoyable to read, whether it is via email, text, or a messaging platform. What makes their writing so effective? What tactics could you use to engage readers of your writing more?

6. Which communication tools (chat, email, text, calls) are you currently using most on your team—and are they working for everyone? What does the team do well when it comes to communication, and where is there room for improvement? How could greater clarity or agreement on when to use each channel improve workflow, increase efficiency, or reduce friction on the team?

7. Describe a recent example of effective data visualization you've seen, either at work or outside of it. Why did it work so well? How could you enhance your ability to tell persuasive stories with charts?

8. How do you tend to feel about presenting or speaking in front of an audience—open or closed, receptive or defensive? Why is that? How do you think these feelings impact your ability to be authentic in this context? What message does your normal body language convey to your audience? How can you connect more authentically with people you're speaking or presenting to?

9. How is psychological safety practiced and modeled on your team? How does your team's level of psychological safety impact creativity, collaboration, and overall performance? What common misconceptions about psychological safety exist in your organization, and how might you go about correcting them?

10. Reflect on the communication challenges of being on a diverse team—particularly one that includes people from different cultures or is spread across the globe. Can you think of times when a message, either written or spoken, landed differently with different groups? What could have been done to make the message more widely understood? What jargon, acronyms, culturally specific references, or buzzwords could your team use less frequently—or cut out altogether—to avoid confusion?

11. What regular practices—like one-on-ones, listening tours, or town halls—do you or your team prioritize that signal an intention to truly listen to people? How often are you

listening without distraction, judgment, or agenda, to understand the other person? What mechanisms can you put in place to ensure that you're hearing fresh ideas with potential and detecting early warning signs of trouble when conversing with team members?

12. Using the lens of creating value for both sides of a negotiation from "What People Still Get Wrong About Negotiations," reexamine a recent deal that might have benefited from this mindset. In what ways does your organizational culture support or inhibit creative deal-making? What tactics could you use to uncover what matters most to the other party? What would change if you consistently approached negotiation as a joint problem-solving exercise rather than a contest?

13. What does courage look like in your organization? Can you think of examples of people speaking up? Whose voices are missing, and why might some people hesitate to express dissent or raise concerns? How can you model courage for others?

14. What other sources on communication have had a significant impact on your work? Were there voices or subtopics you missed in this collection? Were there voices or subtopics included that surprised you?

15. After reading and reflecting on this book, and discussing it with people on your team, write down the ideas and techniques you want to try. Think of how you might experiment and implement those in both the short-term and long-term. Draft a plan to move forward.

Notes

Quick Read: Did You Get My Slack/Email/Text?

1. Erica Dhawan, *The Digital Communication Crisis*, https://ericadhawan
.com/wp-content/uploads/2021/05/The-Digital-Communication-Crisis.pdf.

Quick Read: What's the Best Way to Communicate on a Global Team?

1. Zachariah C. Brown, Eric M. Anicich, and Adam D. Galinsky, "Compensatory Conspicuous Communication: Low Status Increases Jargon Use," *Organizational Behavior and Human Decision Processes* 161 (2020): 274–90.

2. Molly Young, "Garbage Language: Why Do Corporations Speak the Way They Do?," *New York Magazine*, February 17, 2020, https://www.vulture
.com/2020/02/spread-of-corporate-speak.html.

3. Lennox Morrison, "Native English Speakers Are the World's Worst Communicators," BBC, October 31, 2016, https://www.bbc.com/worklife
/article/20161028-native-english-speakers-are-the-worlds-worst-communicators.

Chapter 8: Are You Really a Good Listener?

1. Jeffrey Yip and Colin M. Fisher, "Listening in Organizations: A Synthesis and Future Agenda," *Academy of Management Annals* 16, no. 2 (July 22, 2022), https://journals.aom.org/doi/10.5465/annals.2020.0367.

2. Jason Aten, "Google Just Ended One of Its Longest-Standing Traditions and Forever Changed How It Handles All-Company Meetings," *Inc.*, November 19, 2019, https://www.inc.com/jason-aten/google-just-ended-1-of-its-longest
-standing-traditions-forever-changed-how-it-handles-all-company-meetings
.html.

3. Ted O'Callahan, "What's the Google Approach to Human Capital?," *Yale Insights*, March 17, 2011, https://insights.som.yale.edu/insights/whats-the
-google-approach-to-human-capital.

4. Steven Levy, "Google Shakes Up Its 'TGIF'—and Ends Its Culture of Openness," *Wired*, November 19, 2019, https://www.wired.com/story/google
-shakes-up-its-tgif-and-ends-its-culture-of-openness/.

5. Nitasha Tiku, "Three Years of Misery Inside Google, the Happiest Company in Tech," *Wired*, August 13, 2019, https://www.wired.com/story
/inside-google-three-years-misery-happiest-company-tech/.

6. Cecilia D'Anastasio, "Activision Blizzard Employees Walk Out After Allegations of Rampant Sexism," *Wired*, July 28, 2021, https://www.wired.com/story/activision-blizzard-employees-walk-out-after-allegations-of-rampant-sexism/; Jason Del Rey, "Amazon Often Says Its Employees Are Satisfied. Workers Explain Why You Should Question the Data," *Fortune*, June 12, 2024, https://finance.yahoo.com/news/amazon-often-says-employees-satisfied-213029898.html.

7. Stephanie Mehta, "Exclusive: MillerKnoll CEO Andi Owen Talks RTO and What She Learned from That Infamous Town Hall," *Fast Company*, July 5, 2023, https://www.fastcompany.com/90916660/exclusive-millerknoll-ceo-andi-owen-talks-rto-and-what-she-learned-from-that-infamous-town-hall.

8. Augusto Gnisci et al., "Does Frequency of Interruptions Amplify the Effect of Various Types of Interruptions? Experimental Evidence," *Journal of Nonverbal Behavior* 36, (2012): 39–57, https://doi.org/10.1007/s10919-011-0121-6.

9. Aimee Pichi, "CEO Sparks Backlash After Praising Employee Who Sold Family Dog After Return-to-Office Mandate," CBS News, April 21, 2023, https://www.cbsnews.com/news/clearlink-ceo-video-james-clarke-praises-employee-sold-dog/.

10. G. Itzchakov, A. N. Kluger, and D. R. Castro, "I Am Aware of My Inconsistencies But Can Tolerate Them: The Effect of High Quality Listening on Speakers' Attitude Ambivalence," *Personality and Social Psychology Bulletin* 43, no. 1 (2016): 105–120, https://doi.org/10.1177/0146167216675339.

11. J. B. Bavelas, L. Coates, and T. Johnson, "Listeners as Co-Narrators," *Journal of Personality and Social Psychology* 79, no. 6 (2000): 941–952, https://doi.org/10.1037/0022-3514.79.6.941.

12. Christopher C. Rosen et al., "When Lending an Ear Turns into Mistreatment: An Episodic Examination of Leader Mistreatment in Response to Venting at Work," *Personnel Psychology* 74, no. 1 (2020): 175–195.

13. Johana Bhuiyan, "The Google Walkout: What Protesters Demanded and What They Got," *Los Angeles Times*, November 6, 2019, https://www.latimes.com/business/technology/story/2019-11-06/google-walkout-demands.

14. Michaela Kerrissey et al., "Overcoming Walls and Voids: Responsive Practices That Enable Frontline Workers to Feel Heard," *Health Care Management Review* 49, no. 2 (2024): 116–126.

About the Contributors

Max H. Bazerman is the Jesse Isidor Straus Professor of Business Administration at Harvard Business School. He is the author of several books, including *Inside an Academic Scandal: A Story of Trust and Betrayal* and *Negotiation: The Game Has Changed*.

Scott Berinato is a senior editor at *Harvard Business Review* and the author of *Good Charts Workbook: Tips Tools, and Exercises for Making Better Data Visualizations* (Harvard Business Review Press, 2019) and *Good Charts: The HBR Guide to Making Smarter, More Persuasive Data Visualizations* (Harvard Business Review Press, 2016).

Bill Birchard is a business author and book-writing coach. He is the author of *Writing for Impact: 8 Secrets from Science That Will Fire Up Your Readers' Brains*. His previous books include *Merchants of Virtue, Stairway to Earth, Nature's Keepers, Counting What Counts*, and others.

Alison Wood Brooks is the O'Brien Associate Professor of Business Administration at Harvard Business School, and author of *Talk: The Science of Conversation and the Art of Being Ourselves*.

Dan Bullock is the head of the Language and Communications Programme at the United Nations Secretariat, training diplomats and global UN staff. Dan is the coauthor of *How to Communicate Effectively with Anyone, Anywhere* and has codelivered a TEDx Talk on communications. He has also served as faculty teaching business communication, linguistics, and public relations within the Division of Programs in Business at New York University's School of Professional Studies. He was the director of corporate communications at a leading NYC public relations firm, and his corporate clients have included TD Bank and Pfizer.

John Coleman is the author of the *HBR Guide to Crafting Your Purpose* (Harvard Business Review Press, 2022) and *Good Money* (Harvard Business Review Press, 2026).

Jay A. Conger is the Henry R. Kravis Research Chair in Leadership Studies at Claremont McKenna College. He is coauthor of *The High Potential's Advantage* (Harvard Business Review Press, 2018).

James R. Detert is the John L. Colley Professor of Business Administration at the University of Virginia Darden School of Business, and the author of *Choosing Courage: The Everyday Guide to Being Brave at Work* (Harvard Business Review Press, 2021).

Erica Dhawan is a leading expert on 21st-century teamwork and collaboration. She is an award-winning keynote speaker and the author of the book *Digital Body Language*. Download her free guide, "End Digital Burnout" from ericadhawan.com and follow her on LinkedIn.

Amy C. Edmondson is the Novartis Professor of Leadership and Management at Harvard Business School. Her latest book is *Right Kind of Wrong: The Science of Failing Well*.

Colin M. Fisher is an associate professor and a program director at University College London School of Management and the author of *The Collective Edge: Unlocking the Secret Power of Groups*. He has a PhD from Harvard Business School, and his research focuses on creativity and team dynamics.

Leslie K. John is the James E. Burke Professor of Business Administration at Harvard Business School and author of *Revealing: The Underrated Power of Oversharing*.

Michaela J. Kerrissey is an associate professor of management at the Harvard T.H. Chan School of Public Health.

Nick Morgan is a speaker, coach, and the president and founder of Public Words, a communications consulting firm based in Greater Boston. He is the author of *Can You Hear Me? How to Connect with People in a Virtual World*.

Raúl Sánchez is the director of the NYU Workplace Learning Innovation Lab and an award-winning professor of intercultural business communication at New York University's School of Professional Studies. Raúl is the coauthor of *How to Communicate Effectively with Anyone, Anywhere* and has codelivered a TEDx Talk on communications. He has designed and delivered corporate trainings for Deloitte and the United Nations, and has been a writing consultant for Barnes & Noble Press and PBS. He was awarded the NYU School of Professional Studies Teaching Excellence Award and specializes in linguistics and business communication.

Holly Weeks is an independent consultant and the president of Holly Weeks Communications in Cambridge, Massachusetts.

She is the author of *Failure to Communicate* (Harvard Business Review Press, 2008). She also teaches at the Harvard Kennedy School.

Sarah Noll Wilson is an executive coach, facilitator, and researcher who is on a mission to make the workplace work better for humans. She is the author of *Don't Feed the Elephants!: Overcoming the Art of Avoidance to Build Powerful Partnerships* and host of the weekly podcast *Conversations on Conversations*.

Jeffrey Yip is an associate professor of management at Simon Fraser University, where he teaches leadership in the Executive MBA and executive education programs. He is known for his listen and build approach, which helps leaders drive change by building trust and momentum through listening.

Index